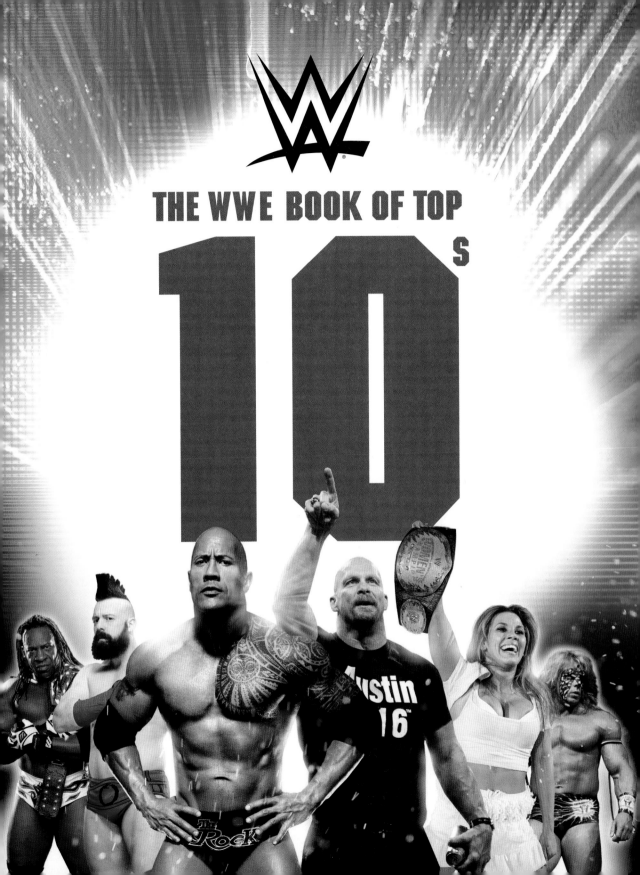

THE WWE BOOK OF TOP 10s

CONTENTS

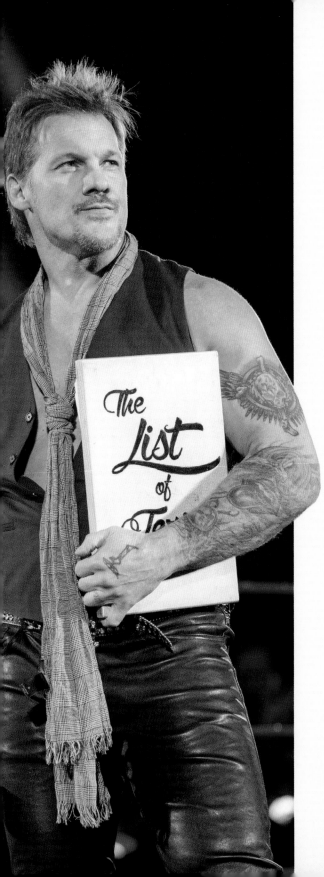

When the muttonheads at WWE Books asked me to write an introduction to this tome, I didn't quite see the point. I mean if they were going to be honest, every list would have "Chris Jericho" as the #1 entry, with my best friend, Kevin Owens at #2, right? But after reading an early copy of this, I'd say some of it is good, but most of it (especially the parts not about me) is useless. So if you are going to buy this pile of crapski, since I am the master and creator of the only List that matters, I thought I'd give you something to make your purchase worth it.

CHRIS JERICHO'S TOP 10 LIST OF THINGS THAT SHOULD GO ON THE LIST OF JERICHO

#1. Stupid idiots

#2. Stores that don't keep $750 pashmina scarves in stock

#3. Dumb idiots

#4. Morons that say they are the greatest Champion in history . . . when it's obvious that the right answer is me. (Even the monkeys at WWE Books know this. Check out page 160)

#5. Barbarians who that think that "sparkle crotch" is funny

#6. Anybody in the WWE Universe who is reading this book instead of one of my four bestselling autobiographies

#7. Dean Ambrose, who was responsible for 69 TACKS piercing my skin, AND who still owes me $15,000!

#8. Ashton Kutcher, who's still going to get . . . IT!

#9. Idiotic idiots

#10. And finally . . . YOU!

TOP 10s
SUPERSTARS

⑧

⑦

1 THE BOOGEYMAN

As if the Boogeyman's sinister painted face and jerky movements weren't frightening enough, the gruesome Superstar would unnerve opponents further by eating live worms—by the handful! He was accompanied to the ring by a miniature version of himself, known as Little Boogeyman.

2 THE DUDLEY FAMILY

Although the WWE Universe thinks of Bubba Ray, D-Von, and Spike as the Dudley Boyz, the trio are just a small part of the Dudley family. Led by Big Dick Dudley, The Dudley Family featured a collection of tie-dye clad half-brothers, including Dudley Dudley, Chubby Dudley, and Snot Dudley.

3 GOLDUST

Dustin Rhodes is better known as Goldust, the outlandish and bizarre Superstar who sported a gold outfit and had been known to gyrate in the ring. His flamboyant style unnerved his opponents in and out of the ring, and won him various titles, including three Intercontinental Championships.

4 HORNSWOGGLE

For more than ten years, WWE had its very own leprechaun: Hornswoggle. His crafty moves, such as his "Sweet Shin Music" knee kick, took down taller opponents. And he even managed to win the WWE Cruiserweight Title. The Superstar was also revealed, incorrectly, to be Mr. McMahon's illegitimate son!

5 THE BROOD

The Brood was a trio of competitors who idolized vampires. The stable—consisting of Gangrel, Edge, and Christian—would arrange "bloodbaths" during matches where the lights would go out and then come back on to reveal the Brood's unfortunate opponents soaked in blood.

TOP 10 OUTRAGEOUS SUPERSTARS

6 VAL VENIS

One of the most controversial Superstars of the Attitude Era, Val Venis brought bawdy behavior and awkward innuendo to his matches and interviews. His brash ring entry involved suggestive moves and an invitation to a member of the crowd to whip off the towel around his waist, revealing his shorts.

7 THE GOBBLEDY GOOKER

In the weeks leading up to *Survivor Series 1990*, a mysterious oversized egg kept appearing at WWE live events. The egg reappeared at *Survivor Series* and finally hatched. A Superstar emerged, dressed bizarrely as a dancing bird named the Gobbledy Gooker.

8 MANTAUR

During 1995, Mantaur intimidated Superstars by entering the ring in an alarming bull's head that covered his upper torso. Once inside the ring, he snorted, stomped, and charged at his opponents. Mantaur won a few matches under the tutelage of his manager, James E. Cornette, before leaving WWE.

9 THE SHOCKMASTER

The Shockmaster competed in WCW and for much of that time he was an average contender. His debut, however was particularly notorious. The Superstar intended to burst through a wall in a helmet, which concealed his identity. But he tripped and fell through the wall instead, losing his helmet in the process!

10 DAMIEN DEMENTO

Claiming to be from "The Outer Reaches of Your Mind," Demento was a difficult competitor to face. He often acted in strange and disturbing ways, such as speaking to people that were not in the ring. Demento saw some early success, but left WWE within a year.

SPORTS ENTERTAINMENT has included over-the-top and larger-than-life personalities throughout its history. But some Superstars have amped up the levels of strange and unusual in ways that have shocked as well as entertained the WWE Universe.

7

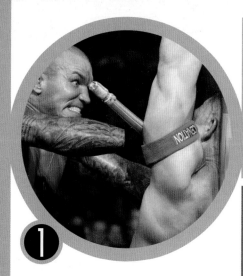

1 RANDY ORTON

By far, John Cena's longest-running rivalry has been with Randy Orton. Both Cena and Orton joined WWE in 2002, and both became main event competitors and highly decorated champions, with Cena holding 15 world championship titles and Orton reigning as world champion 12 times.

1

2 EDGE

By winning the first *Money in the Bank* match at *WrestleMania 21*, Edge earned the right to challenge for a championship. He capitalized at *New Year's Revolution 2006* and pinned the exhausted Champ. Cena regained the title later in the month, but the two battled constantly over the next few years.

2

3 BATISTA

Comparisons between John Cena and Batista began when they each won their first world championships at *WrestleMania 21*. After Batista pinned Cena to capture the WWE Championship in 2010, the two met in several matches, culminating in Batista saying "I Quit" in a match at *Over the Limit*.

4 CM PUNK

By July 2011, CM Punk was sick of what he thought was favorable treatment of John Cena by WWE management. Punk took out his anger at *Money in the Bank 2011* and beat Cena for the WWE Championship. Punk later won another WWE Championship match against Cena at *SummerSlam 2011*.

5 THE ROCK

After John Cena questioned The Rock's commitment to WWE, the two began a heated war of words. The Superstars finally took their quarrel into the ring at *WrestleMania XXVIII*. The Rock won the match, but Cena got his revenge a year later in 2013 when he pinned The Rock for the WWE Championship.

TOP 10 JOHN CENA RIVALS

6 CHRIS JERICHO

John Cena's first pay-per-view win came at the expense of Chris Jericho in 2002. Jericho tried to get his revenge. In 2005, he failed to capture the World Championship from Cena in numerous matches. *RAW* manager, Eric Bischoff, finally fired Jericho after he lost a Last Chance Match to Cena on *RAW*.

7 KURT ANGLE

John Cena's first rivalry was with Kurt Angle. In 2002, Angle challenged anyone listening backstage to face him. Cena, who had never competed in WWE, accepted and almost won the bout. Angle targeted him in 2005 when Cena was WWE Champion, but Cena retained his title.

8 BROCK LESNAR

In 2003, John Cena's first WWE Championship Match saw him lose to Brock Lesnar. Almost 10 years later, the two met in an Extreme Rules Match. Cena won, despite Lesnar's power. At *SummerSlam 2014*, they met again, with Cena's WWE Championship at stake. Lesnar won with a truly dominant performance.

9 ERIC BISCHOFF

After winning his first WWE Championship, John Cena was drafted to the *RAW* roster. General Manager Eric Bischoff wanted the Champ as an ally against the resurgent ECW. Cena refused to help, so Bischoff tried to take Cena's Championship by aiding his challengers, but his attempts got him fired.

10 AJ STYLES

When AJ Styles joined WWE in 2016, the WWE Universe couldn't wait to watch the newcomer and John Cena clash. At first, the two seemed to have a respectful rivalry, but animosity grew. Styles beat Cena at *Money in the Bank 2016* and *SummerSlam 2016*.

JOHN CENA HAS BEEN the face of WWE since 2004. His position has made him extremely popular with the WWE Universe, but it has also made him a target for every other Superstar. Whether chasing a championship or just breaking through, John Cena tends to bring out the best in his competition.

TOP 10
CANADIAN SUPERSTARS

Some of the most storied Superstars in sports entertainment history have come from Canada.

1 BRET "HIT MAN" HART This Hall of Famer hailed from Calgary, Alberta, and held every major championship in his WWE and WCW tenures.

2 EDGE From Orangeville, Ontario, Edge is one of the most decorated Superstars in WWE history with more than 30 championships.

3 TRISH STRATUS Hailing from Toronto, Stratus was a seven-time Women's Champion and was named Diva of the Decade in 2003.

4 CHRIS JERICHO Jericho grew up in Winnipeg and has won dozens of titles around the world, most notably becoming WWE's first Undisputed Champion.

5 RICK MARTEL Born in Quebec City, Rick Martel won singles and tag team championships in WWE and around the world.

6 NATALYA A third-generation Superstar from the Hart family of Calgary, Natalya became the Divas Champion in 2010.

7 OWEN HART Also a member of the Hart family, Owen is considered one of the greatest WWE Superstars ever.

8 MAD DOG VACHON From Montreal, Hall of Famer Vachon won the AWA World Heavyweight Champion five times during his 36-year-long career.

9 CHRISTIAN Born in Kitchener, Ontario, Christian won the WWE Tag Team Championship seven times with his best friend Edge, and carved out a successful singles career.

10 PAT PATTERSON Hailing from Montreal, Patterson was a successful wrestler, as well as a key figure in the global development of WWE.

TOP 10 CROSSOVER SPORTS STARS

Athletes from other sporting backgrounds have stepped into the WWE ring.

1 KURT ANGLE Angle won Olympic gold for the U.S. in freestyle wrestling at the 1996 Summer Olympic Games.

2 ERNIE LADD Ladd played professional football for the San Diego Chargers for most of the 1960s.

3 BROCK LESNAR Brock Lesnar won UFC's World Heavyweight Championship and then came back to WWE to win the WWE World Heavyweight Championship once again.

4 WAHOO MCDANIEL McDaniel played professional football for the Houston Oilers, Denver Broncos, New York Jets, and Miami Dolphins from 1960 to 1968.

5 MARK HENRY Henry twice represented the U.S. in weightlifting at the Summer Olympic Games in 1992 and 1996.

6 RON SIMMONS Simmons played professional football in three leagues: the NFL, USFL, and the CFL.

7 KEVIN NASH Nash played basketball at the University of Tennessee, and for various professional teams in Europe.

8 KEN SHAMROCK A mixed-martial arts pioneer, Shamrock headlined seven of the first nine UFC events.

9 KEN PATERA In 1972, Patera represented the U.S. in weightlifting, at the Summer Olympic Games in Munich.

10 ROMAN REIGNS He played for the Georgia Tech Yellow Jackets and subsequently signed to a number of professional teams, most successfully the CFL's Edmonton Eskimos.

Olympic gold medalist and WWE Champion, Kurt Angle

Trish Stratus (left); Bret "Hit Man" Hart (above)

TOP 10

THE ROCK'S VERBAL SMACKDOWNS

THROUGHOUT HIS career, The Rock developed an arsenal of jaw-dropping insults to hurl at opponents. No matter what he says, The Rock always delights the WWE Universe and shocks the competition with his biting put-downs.

1 IT DOESN'T MATTER...

The Rock really knows how to get into his opponents' heads before a match when he pretends not to know their names—or even care. The Rock's "it doesn't matter" burn always catches his foes off guard and crushes their confidence, giving him an advantage.

2 INTERVIEW INSULTS

In December 2000, during a pre-match interview for the WWE Championship, The Rock imitated all five of his opponents. He mocked Rikishi, calling him a "thong-wearing fatty." He also had some choice words for the WWE Chairman's daughter, Stephanie McMahon.

3 KNOW YOUR ROLE...

The Rock has always aimed to put his competitors in their place. He often tells his opponents to "know your role and shut your mouth." No one has been spared from this directive, from Superstars to announcers to authority figures.

4 A BAD GAME

Triple H—The Rock's rival—nicknamed himself "The Game" to imply that sports entertainment would be nothing without him. In August 1999 before a *SmackDown* match, The Rock told The Game that he needed to go back to the drawing board because ". . . your game absolutely sucks!"

5 33-POUND HEAD

Most Superstars in WWE were either too afraid or too respectful to insult the menacing Undertaker and face his supernatural powers—but The Rock was not a typical Superstar. The Rock mocked The Undertaker regularly, once targeting his "Mickey Mouse tattoos and 33-pound head."

6 "FRUITY PEBBLES™"

After a seven-year absence, The Rock was announced as guest host of *WrestleMania XXVII*. He immediately took aim at John Cena, ridiculing his wardrobe choices and remarking that his collection of brightly colored t-shirts made Cena look like "a big fat bowl of Fruity Pebbles!"

7 HAIRCUT-DOWN

In 2002, The Rock commented on massive Superstar Big Show's new haircut, saying that he went from a "long-haired, seven-foot, 500-pound piece of monkey crap" to a "short-haired, seven-foot, 500-pound piece of steaming, stinking, Grade-A monkey crap."

8 CLASS ACT

The Rock aimed to insult the intelligence of his rival Booker T before their WCW Championship Match. The Rock told fans that when Booker T was in school, Booker's teacher asked what two plus two equalled, and young Booker confidently answered, "Thomas Jefferson, sucka!"

9 SMACKDOWN SONG

No one is safe from The Rock's insults—not even the WWE Universe! In March 2003, The Rock played the guitar and serenaded a Sacramento, California audience. The Rock sang that they were crazy to live there and put down their basketball team, the Sacramento Kings, to a chorus of boos.

10 JABRONI

The Rock loves to throw the word "jabroni"—which took on a meaning similar to "loser"—around to rile up his opponents. Others have used this insult to diminish another competitor's skills, but not with the same impact.

THE ROCK

"KNOW YOUR ROLE AND SHUT YOUR MOUTH, JABRONI."

10

TOP 10

RKOS

RANDY ORTON CREATED a new signature finishing move in 2003, naming it the RKO (from the initials of his full name—Randal Keith Orton). In an RKO, Orton catches his opponent in a three-quarter facelock, then falls backward, forcing them to the mat. The RKO became a frequent match-winning move for Orton.

1 EVAN BOURNE

While Evan Bourne was not a longtime rival, he was the victim of one of Orton's most spectacular RKOs. With Orton down on the mat, Bourne flipped off the top rope. Quick as a flash, a seemingly floored Orton sprang up and caught the flying Bourne in an RKO.

2 JOHN CENA

When Cena and Orton fought at *TLC: Tables, Ladders, and Chairs 2013*, Orton knocked Cena off a ladder and promptly delivered an RKO, allowing Orton to win the match and unify the WWE Championship and the World Heavyweight Championship.

3 CHRISTIAN

In 2011, Randy Orton and Christian fought in a steel cage on *SmackDown*. Christian tried to climb out of the cage, which would have resulted in a win. Unfortunately for Christian, Orton caught him and then punished him with a devastating RKO.

4 TRIPLE H

Triple H received his share of RKOs during his many heated battles with Orton. At *No Mercy 2007*, Triple H tried to take out Orton on the TV announcer's desk. Orton delivered an RKO to Triple H, slamming him onto the desk. Randy won the match—and broke the desk.

5 CACTUS JACK

At *Backlash 2004*, Randy Orton and Cactus Jack fought in a brutal match for the Intercontinental Championship. Orton destroyed Cactus Jack by RKO-ing him onto Jack's own barbed wire-wrapped baseball bat, ending the match and retaining the Intercontinental Championship Title.

6 UNDERTAKER

At *WrestleMania 21*, Randy Orton became the 13th Superstar to fall during Undertaker's *WrestleMania* 21-0 winning streak. Still, Orton impressed everyone when he turned a potentially match-ending slam to the mat by Undertaker into a punishing RKO.

7

7 CM PUNK

CM Punk and Orton clashed at *WrestleMania XXVII*. Punk decided to try his luck with a high-risk maneuver, coming off the top rope to catch Orton by the neck and knock him down with a devastating Clothesline. Instead, Orton caught Punk midair and reversed the move into an RKO, ending the match.

8 DOLPH ZIGGLER

During an episode of *RAW* in 2014, Ziggler leaped at his opponent, wrapping his legs around Orton's neck in an attempt to knock him down. But Orton grabbed Ziggler's legs, tossed him into the air, and pulled him into a match-winning RKO that sent Ziggler slamming to the mat face-first.

"THIS IS NOT GOOD FOR DOLPH ZIGGLER!"
WWE COMMENTATOR

9 JEFF HARDY

The charismatic Jeff Hardy hoped to take the WWE Championship from Randy Orton at the 2008 *Royal Rumble*. Hardy looked set for victory, and tried to end the match with his signature move, the Twist of Fate. But Orton countered with an impressive RKO and pinned Hardy.

8

10 SETH ROLLINS

Following an attack by Orton on Rollins after *Fastlane 2015*, the two faced off in a main event match at *WrestleMania 31*. With Orton doubled over, Rollins tried to take advantage. But Randy sprang up suddenly, converting Rollins' attempt into an epic, high-flying RKO.

TOP 10 POWERFUL WOMEN

FEMALE SUPERSTARS bring a variety of skills and abilities to sports entertainment. Over the years, the women of WWE have used their talent and strength to overwhelm the competition, dominate in the ring, and impress the WWE Universe.

1 CHYNA

Chyna debuted in WWE as a bodyguard for the villainous Triple H. A true pioneer, Chyna became the first woman to challenge for, and win, the Intercontinental Championship and participate in a Royal Rumble Match and a King of the Ring tournament—all against male competitors.

2 NICOLE BASS

Nicole Bass made her WWE debut as the glamorous Sable's bodyguard at *WrestleMania XV*. During her time in WWE, the former championship bodybuilder terrorized most of WWE's female Superstars, and a few of the male ones, too, with punishing slams delivered by her muscular frame.

3 BETH PHOENIX

Three-time Women's Champion Beth Phoenix was a powerhouse competitor during her days in WWE. She used her incredible strength to lift opponents high above her head and slam them down on the mat. She also eliminated the 400-pound Great Khali from the 2010 Royal Rumble Match.

4 SHANIQUA

Shaniqua managed the Basham Brothers in 2003 and 2004, often using her fierce disposition to protect her charges. In singles matches, she shocked other female competitors with her signature Lariat Clothesline move as her powerful swinging arm swiftly brought the competition to the mat.

5 ALUNDRA BLAYZE

Alundra Blayze was one of the most talented female competitors from the 1980s to the 1990s. The Hall of Famer suplexed her competition, lifting them up and throwing them down to the mat, to win titles in WWE, WCW, AWA, and Japan.

6 ASYA

From 1999 to 2000, Asya was an intimidating presence in WCW. Originally the valet for the Revolution faction, the powerful Asya competed against women and men. She famously fought in tag team matches against the male tag team, Filthy Animals.

7 JAZZ

Jazz made her sports entertainment debut with ECW and defeated Jason of the Impact Players at *Heat Wave 1999*. She moved to WWE and became a powerful adversary, winning the Women's Championship twice in her career.

8 STEPHANIE MCMAHON

Wielding the power of her family's standing in WWE, as well as her keen business sense, Stephanie McMahon has risen to a commanding position in the company, running both *RAW* and *SmackDown* at different times in her career.

9 BERTHA FAYE

In 1995, Bertha Faye used her size and strength to power her way to a two-month reign as Women's Champion. Faye was also able to use her skill and power to defeat fierce competitor Alundra Blayze for the title at *SummerSlam 1995*.

10 NIA JAX

After joining WWE in 2016, Nia Jax immediately made an impact, beginning a lengthy winning streak. Jax has overwhelmed her opponents with power slams and clubbing blows that leave them begging for mercy.

CHYNA

"THE NINTH WONDER OF THE WORLD GETS ANYTHING SHE WANTS."

1 REY MYSTERIO

This legendary masked Superstar has worn hundreds of variations of his mask. Each honors the Mexican wrestling warriors of the past in its design.

2 MIL MÁSCARAS

Debuting in 1965, Máscaras was the first masked Superstar to wrestle at Madison Square Garden in New York, where mask-wearing was illegal until 1972.

3 KANE

Kane joined WWE with a chilling red mask, ostensibly covering burns sustained in childhood.

4 JUSHIN "THUNDER" LIGER

Known for his skillful aerial moves, Liger joined WCW in 1991, sporting a crazy anime-style mask with five jagged horns and printed fangs.

5 MANKIND

The deranged Superstar Mankind wore a brown leather mask that looked more like a muzzle, reflecting his disturbing persona.

6 ULTIMO DRAGON

Ultimo donned a dramatic costume and mask inspired by both Mexican wrestling and his native Japan.

7 VADER

Also known as "The Mastodon," Vader's iconic red mask adds to his prehistoric beast persona.

TOP 10
MASKED
SUPERSTARS

MANY COMPETITORS have enhanced their appearance by wearing masks. Some have worn coverings designed to intimidate their opponents, while others have worn colorful masks to celebrate their culture and history.

SIN CARA

8 ▶

Mexican Superstar Sin Cara, whose name means "without face," opts for a mysterious design that covers his entire face.

▲

10 THE PATRIOT

The Patriot honored the United States with a mask featuring stars, stripes, and an eagle.

◀ 9 **THE HURRICANE**

Green-haired and masked, the Hurricane stood for justice in the ring. His comic-book style mask was the perfect fit for his righteous superhero persona.

TOP 10
SUPERSTAR TATTOOS

Many of the biggest Superstars have had meaningful tattoos.

1 BROCK LESNAR
The evil-looking demon tattoo on the monstrous Lesnar's back strikes fear into anyone that meets him in the ring.

2 BAM BAM BIGELOW The flames on Bigelow's scalp matched his ring gear and made him look even more aggressive.

3 BATISTA The sprawling fire-breathing dragon on Batista's back intimidated his competitors and represented his power.

4 LITA Successful Superstar Lita showed off her sinister side with the three-eyed demon tattoo on her right arm.

5 THE ROCK The symbols on The Rock's tribal tattoo represent many things, including his success, his struggles, and his loyalty to his family.

6 ROMAN REIGNS Covering his entire right arm, Roman Reigns' battle tattoo extends out of his flak jacket and looks like a powerful weapon.

7 JEFF HARDY The tree roots weaving up his right arm make Hardy feel connected to the Earth.

8 GOLDBERG Goldberg's tribal tattoo represents his strength and power—and acted as a warning.

9 UNDERTAKER The demons and skulls on Undertaker's arms acknowledge his deathly, supernatural aura.

10 REY MYSTERIO Mexican-Amercian Mysterio's angel wings match his signature luchador mask and reflect the grooves of the Aztec calendar.

Naomi wore this colorful outfit in August 2016.

TOP 10
BEST DRESSED

Some Superstars are remembered for their in-ring fashions.

1 RICK RUDE Rick Rude wore some memorable airbrushed tights throughout his career, but none topped the pair that boasted the face of rival Jake Roberts' wife.

2 TED DIBIASE The "Million Dollar Man" showed off his wealth by wearing a black-and-gold tuxedo with dollar signs embroidered on both lapels.

3 JUSHIN "THUNDER" LIGER Wearing a red-white-and-blue body suit with a horned mask and a silver sequined cape, Liger looked like a superhero in the ring.

4 HILLBILLY JIM The popular Superstar stood out by competing in matches dressed in blue jean overalls.

5 MISS ELIZABETH The valet wore classy cocktail dresses and evening gowns in the ring.

6 GORGEOUS GEORGE In the 1940s and 1950s, Gorgeous George impressed the crowds with his lacy sequined robes.

7 BIG BOSS MAN Big Boss Man dressed as a corrections officer, with a collared blue shirt, dark pants, and badges.

8 MVP The cocky Superstar's sporty singlet was designed to make him look like a world-class athlete.

9 NAOMI Naomi often wears eye-catching outfits in bright, glowing fluorescent colors.

10 TUGBOAT The best friend of Hulk Hogan looked more fit for the high seas than the ring with his red-and-white striped captain's shirt and white sailor pants.

The Rock (left); Bam Bam Bigelow (above)

TOP 10 BIGGEST CRYBABIES

NO ONE EVER WANTS TO lose in sports entertainment, but some competitors take it harder than others. Some whine about how they were wronged, or insist that they were double-crossed by their opponents, the officials, and even the WWE Universe.

1 BIG SHOW

Big Show was forced to beg for forgiveness in May 2012 when *RAW* General Manager, John Laurinaitis, failed to see the funny side of Big Show's imitation of his raspy voice. Big Show dropped to his knees, apologizing and sobbing uncontrollably, but he was fired.

2 1-2-3 KID

To settle a feud between 1-2-3 Kid and Razor Ramon, WWE's one-time only Crybaby Match was held in February 1996 in which the loser of the match would be forced to wear a diaper! Ramon managed to pin the 1-2-3 Kid and put a diaper on him—to Kid's eternal embarrassment.

3 BRET "HIT MAN" HART

After years of being admired as a hero, Bret "Hit Man" Hart's popularity declined when he criticized WWE's extreme new direction in the Attitude Era. Blaming this direction on American fans, in 1997 patriotic Canadian Hart went as far as reviving the Hart Foundation as an anti-American stable.

4 STEPHANIE MCMAHON

Long before becoming the confident executive that represents WWE today, Stephanie McMahon was infamous for her screeching fits when events didn't play out as she'd hoped. Her tears flowed in spectacular fashion in 2002 when Triple H left her at the altar on *RAW*.

5 CHRISTIAN

After a series of defeats in 2002, a frustrated Christian began to lash out the way a petulant toddler would. When Diamond Dallas Page beat him for the European Championship at *WrestleMania X8*, Christian didn't simply cry, he kicked, thrashed, and pounded the mat.

6 CHRIS JERICHO

Jericho has never been a gracious loser. When Dean Malenko defeated him for the Cruiserweight Championship at *Slamboree 1998*, Jericho claimed Malenko's win was a "conspiracy" designed to relieve him of the Title. Jericho even walked around Washington D.C. holding a "conspiracy victim" sign.

7 BOB BACKLUND

The legendary Bob Backlund returned to the WWE rings in 1992 with a grudge that had been building up for almost 10 years. He insisted that he had not legitimately lost the WWE Championship a decade earlier and that he deserved to be the champion.

1

8 THE MIZ

Throughout late 2016, The Miz made it clear that he felt "overlooked and underappreciated" by WWE General Manager, Daniel Bryan. On an installment of *Talking Smack*, The Miz lost his cool after Bryan suggested he performed like a coward. The Miz's voice and body quivered with rage.

10

9 TRIPLE H

Counter to his well-deserved tough-guy reputation, Triple H threw a tantrum in April 2000 when Chris Jericho won the WWE Championship, blaming it on a fast count in Jericho's favor. Triple H attacked the official, forced him to reverse his decision, and even had the initial decision struck from the record.

10 SIMON DEAN

In 2005, Simon Dean was unable to put on a brave face when confronted with a terrifying opponent: The Boogeyman. Dean was so petrified by the creepy Superstar, he had to be dragged to the ring by a team of security guards.

TOP 10
BEST NICKNAMES

Many Superstars have colorful nicknames that reflect their oversized personalities.

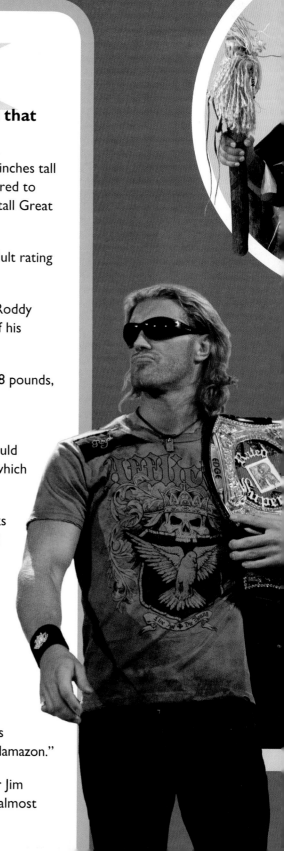

1 **"THE EIGHTH WONDER OF THE WORLD"** At 7-feet 4-inches tall and 520 pounds, Andre the Giant's huge size was compared to the seven wonders of the world, including the 455-foot-tall Great Pyramid of Giza.

2 **"THE RATED R SUPERSTAR"** Edge gave himself an adult rating for his foul language and violent antics in the ring.

3 **"MR. WONDERFUL"** Paul Orndorff's then manager, Roddy Piper, referred to Orndorff as Mr. Wonderful because of his near-perfect physique—and the name stuck.

4 **"THE WALKING CONDOMINIUM"** Weighing in at 458 pounds, King Kong Bundy looked like an indestructible building to his competitors.

5 **"THE DIRTIEST PLAYER IN THE GAME"** Ric Flair would do anything to win and he was no stranger to cheating, which won him this name.

6 **"THE DOGFACED GREMLIN"** With fierce canine looks and an attitude to match, Rick Steiner always intimidated his opponents.

7 **"THE BILLION DOLLAR PRINCESS"** Early in her WWE career, *RAW* Commissioner Stephanie McMahon was given this nickname as the heir to her father Vince's WWE throne.

8 **"THE ICEMAN"** Dean Malenko's cold, calculating demeanor earned him this nickname.

9 **"THE GLAMAZON"** Beth Phoenix was both glamorous and powerful in the ring, so she nicknamed herself "The Glamazon."

10 **"THE CEREBRAL ASSASSIN"** Legendary announcer Jim Ross coined this term for Triple H, who could outsmart almost any opponent.

Mysterious Superstar Papa Shango dressed like a voodoo witch doctor.

TOP 10
SUPERSTARS FROM PARTS UNKNOWN

Some strange Superstars have kept their places of birth shrouded in mystery.

1 ULTIMATE WARRIOR He has a home in the WWE Hall of Fame, but no one knows where Ultimate Warrior is originally from.

2 DEMOLITION Tag team teammates Ax and Smash of Demolition never revealed their hometowns.

3 THE WARLORD He teamed with Barbarian to challenge fellow parts-unknown denizens, Demolition, for the World Tag Team Championships.

4 PAPA SHANGO No one knows where the mystical Superstar, with skull face paint and voodoo practices, is from.

5 THE MISSING LINK Manager Bobby "The Brain" Heenan would not give the slightest clue as to where he found the bizarre competitor known as The Missing Link.

6 DOINK THE CLOWN It would be nice to know where this terrifying clown hailed from—if only to avoid ever visiting his hometown!

7 ZEUS This menacing figure crossed over from the silver screen to the ring to try and exact his revenge on Hulk Hogan.

8 AVATAR The masked Superstar had a regular home with WWE, but he never gave up any clues about his origins.

9 THE BERZERKER The proper question for this Viking-styled Superstar isn't where he came from, but when.

10 BASTIAN BOOGER This odd Superstar was around for just one year. No one knows where he came from—or where he went next.

The "Rated R Superstar," Edge (left) and "The Dogfaced Gremlin," Rick Steiner (above)

TOP 10
BIGGEST RIVALRIES

SPORTS ENTERTAINMENT brings out the competitive drive in all Superstars. When two Superstars seek to achieve the same goal, they often have to battle repeatedly. Some of the deepest rivalries are not just for championships—they also have a personal component.

1 STONE COLD STEVE AUSTIN & MR. MCMAHON

When Stone Cold Steve Austin won the WWE Championship at *WrestleMania XIV*, Mr. McMahon decided that if Austin was going to be the face of WWE, he would have to present a more corporate image. Austin resisted and a bitter conflict between the Champion and Chairman began, lasting several years and producing many of WWE's most indelible moments.

2 BRET HART & SHAWN MICHAELS

From the late 80s and early-to-mid 90s, the careers of Bret Hart and Shawn Michaels ran in close parallel. The two broke into WWE in tag teams, then became singles competitors who competed for the Intercontinental Championship and the WWE Championship. Hart and Michaels were in direct opposition at each step, which resulted in show-stealing matches and personal hatred.

3 RAW & NITRO

Fans of sports entertainment have considered WWE *RAW* prime viewing since it debuted in 1993, but Mondays were even more entertaining starting in 1995 when WCW's *Monday Nitro* debuted. The two shows engaged in five years of intense competition, with Superstars jumping from one show to the other and both WCW and WWE going to great lengths to be the more exciting show.

SHAWN MICHAELS

"HIT MAN, I'M GONNA KNOCK YOU DOWN AND DRAG YOU OUT!"

4 UNDERTAKER & KANE

The most intense sibling rivalry in history took place over almost two decades between Undertaker and his half-brother Kane. Alternately fighting together, against common enemies, or each other, the two Superstars engaged in spectacular matches, including two *WrestleMania* bouts both won by Undertaker.

5 TRIPLE H & THE ROCK

The hostility between Triple H and The Rock stretched through the late 1990s and early 2000s. Each led a dominant faction—The Rock led the Nation of Domination and Triple H led D-Generation X. The two Superstars traded the WWE Championship title four times in early 2000. Their rivalry reared up in 2015 when the two engaged in a verbal battle at *WrestleMania 31*.

CONTINUED

6 THE VON ERICHS & THE FABULOUS FREEBIRDS

Michael Hayes of the faction the Fabulous Freebirds was a special referee for Kerry Von Erich's cage match against NWA Champion Ric Flair. Hayes sneakily tried to help his friend win the Title, but Von Erich refused to win that way. Fellow Freebird Terry Gordy slammed the cage door on Von Erich, allowing Flair to retain the Title and launching a rivalry between the Freebirds and the Von Erich brothers. The rivalry ended when the Von Erich brothers defeated the Freebirds in a "Loser Leaves Texas" Match.

7 TOMMY DREAMER & RAVEN

Raven joined ECW with a specific goal in mind—revenge against his childhood rival, Tommy Dreamer. He even tracked down a girl that he claimed Dreamer had bullied as a child to further torment him. Dreamer finally beat his antagonist at a "Loser Leaves ECW" Match in 1997.

8 EDDIE GUERRERO & REY MYSTERIO

Eddie Guerrero and Rey Mysterio fought over unusual stakes at *SummerSlam 2005*. Guerrero claimed that he was the biological father of Mysterio's son Dominick, so the two had a Ladder Match with custody of Dominick at stake. Mysterio grabbed the dangling custody papers, keeping his family together.

9 HULK HOGAN & RODDY PIPER

Pop singer Cyndi Lauper tried to present an award to manager Captain Lou Albano, but Roddy Piper attacked Albano and Hulk Hogan saved him. This started an extended rivalry and Piper challenged Hogan for the WWE Championship. But when Piper, Paul Orndorff, and "Cowboy" Bob Orton tried to attack the Hulkster, Hogan's friend Mr. T intervened, setting the stage for the first *WrestleMania*.

10 SAMI ZAYN & KEVIN OWENS

Sami Zayn and Kevin Owens were friends and occasional rivals in the ring. When Zayn captured the NXT Championship, Owens, who Zayn thought was his friend at the time, came out to celebrate. But instead of congratulating his friend, Owens attacked Zayn and injured him—making it easier for Owens to take the Title. Both Superstars eventually moved to the main roster, where their rivalry continued.

2

5

3.30.1998

1 MR. MCMAHON

Despite being Stone Cold's boss, WWE Chairman Mr. McMahon has been on the receiving end of numerous Stone Cold Stunners. One of these came when Mr. McMahon demanded that Austin clean up his act and improve his behavior as WWE Champion. Austin let a devastating Stunner serve as his reply.

3.28.1999

2 THE ROCK

The Rock entered *WrestleMania XV* as the Corporate Champion, and Austin was looking to regain the Title from him. Mr. McMahon tried to stack the deck against Stone Cold Steve Austin, but Austin finished off The Rock with a Stone Cold Stunner to win the match and the Championship.

3.29.1998

3 SHAWN MICHAELS

Stone Cold Steve Austin used his patented move to win his first WWE Championship at *WrestleMania XIV*. He nailed champion Shawn Michaels with a Stone Cold Stunner, with special ringside enforcer Mike Tyson making the three-count to award him the victory.

3.14.2004

4 BROCK LESNAR & GOLDBERG

At *WrestleMania XX*, Brock Lesnar and Goldberg met in a grudge match, but with both men leaving WWE after the show, the crowd favorite in the match was special guest referee Stone Cold Steve Austin. They erupted when he took both competitors down with Stone Cold Stunners.

2.23.2003

5 ERIC BISCHOFF

Years after Eric Bischoff fired Stone Cold Steve Austin from WCW, Austin found the ideal opportunity to gain a measure of revenge. He did more than even the score by delivering a stunning sequence of Stone Cold Stunners to Bischoff during a match at *No Way Out 2003*.

6 UNDERTAKER

8.30.1998

Stone Cold Steve Austin defended the WWE Championship against Undertaker in an epic match at *SummerSlam 1998*. Undertaker looked set to win, but Austin countered Undertaker's Old School finishing move into a low blow and a Stone Cold Stunner to pin Undertaker and keep the Title.

7 KURT ANGLE

10.8.2001

Former Olympic wrestler Kurt Angle and Stone Cold were rivals competing over the WWE Championship in the fall of 2001. Angle took the Title at *Unforgiven*, but a rematch on *RAW* two weeks later saw Austin nail Angle with a Stone Cold Stunner to regain the Title.

8 TRIPLE H

5.16.1999

Austin finished off opponents all over the world with his Stone Cold Stunner. Defending the WWE Championship in Manchester, England, in a Triple Threat Match against Undertaker and Triple H, he retained the Title by unleashing a Stone Cold Stunner on Triple H and pinning him.

9 JAKE "THE SNAKE" ROBERTS

6.23.1996

Austin, "The Texas Rattlesnake," began his meteoric rise in WWE by winning the 1996 *King of the Ring* tournament, defeating another snake along the way. WWE Legend Jake "The Snake" Roberts became one of his victims in the finals, leveled by Austin with a decisive Stone Cold Stunner.

10 DONALD TRUMP

4.1.2007

Stone Cold was Special Guest Referee during *WrestleMania 23's* Battle of the Billionaires. He gleefully helped Donald Trump and Bobby Lashley to shave his rival Mr. McMahon's head—then he delivered a Stone Cold Stunner to Trump!

MUCH OF STONE COLD Steve Austin's success was due to his signature move: the Stone Cold Stunner. With a kick, spin, grab, and drop, Austin would knock out competitors, bringing matches to a decisive end. And when his in-ring career ended, the Stunner didn't— Austin still uses it on anyone he feels deserves it!

TOP 10

THORNS IN MR. McMAHON'S SIDE

MR. MCMAHON IS UNDOUBTEDLY the most powerful man in sports entertainment. Many employees and rivals have held longstanding grudges against Mr. McMahon, and on occasion they do get the better of him. But Mr. McMahon continues to run WWE the way he sees fit—and he doesn't care who disagrees with him.

Mr. McMahon and his son, Shane McMahon

"DO NOT CROSS THE BOSS."

MR. MCMAHON

1 STONE COLD STEVE AUSTIN

Between 1998 and 2001, Mr. McMahon tried and failed to end Austin's seemingly unbeatable championship reign.

2 SHANE MCMAHON

Father and son settled a family disagreement in a brutal Street Fight at *WrestleMania X-Seven*.

3 BRET "HIT MAN" HART

After McMahon double-crossed Hart in 1997, Hart got his revenge thirteen years later at *WrestleMania XXVII*.

4 D-GENERATION X

Sick of McMahon's power, Shawn Michaels and Triple H teamed up as D-Generation X to defeat him and his son.

5 HULK HOGAN

Hogan and McMahon fought at *WrestleMania XIX* over who was responsible for WWE's growth since the 80s.

6 RIC FLAIR

Flair and McMahon fought in a spectacular Street Fight at the 2002 *Royal Rumble* for control of WWE.

7 STEPHANIE MCMAHON

Stephanie betrayed her own father by marrying Triple H and helping him defeat McMahon at 1999's *Armageddon*.

8 ERIC BISCHOFF

Eric Bischoff attacked by scheduling his WCW show *Monday Nitro* to clash with WWE's *Monday Night RAW*.

9 MANKIND

Although Mankind tried to cheer up a hospitalized McMahon with a Mr. Socko puppet, he only enraged him.

10 BOBBY LASHLEY

After Donald Trump's representative Bobby Lashley beat Mr. McMahon's Umaga, Trump shaved McMahon bald!

TOP 10 INSANE MICK FOLEY MOMENTS

1 HELL IN A CELL

In one of the most infamous clashes in WWE history, Mankind and Undertaker faced off in a Hell in a Cell Match in 1998 that could have ended Mankind's career. In the brutal match, Mankind was thrown off the top of the cage and later slammed through the cage's roof to the ring below.

2 FLAMING TABLE

Edge and Mick Foley met in a Hardcore Match at *WrestleMania 22*. Before the bout, Edge mocked Foley's status as a Hardcore Legend, stating that *he* would be the Legend after the match. To drive his point home, he speared Foley through a table that Edge's girlfriend, Lita, had set on fire.

3 HARDCORE MATCH

Goaded into facing Randy Orton at *Backlash 2004*, Foley agreed to the bout if it was a Hardcore Match for the Intercontinental Championship. The match featured "Barbie," Mick Foley's barbed-wire wrapped baseball bat, but it backfired, as Orton pulled Foley down onto the bat, pinning him to win the match.

4 AMNESIA

Between 1993 and 1994, Cactus Jack and Big Van Vader clashed. In an April 1993 match, Vader dished out so much punishment that Cactus Jack did not compete for weeks. But the fans of WCW learned that Cactus Jack was temporarily institutionalized and even developed amnesia, forgetting his identity.

5 ON THE ROPES

The rivalry between Cactus Jack and Big Van Vader reached across the Atlantic Ocean. The two clashed in Germany in March 1994, and Cactus Jack got his head tangled in the ropes. The tightly set ropes were almost impossible for Cactus to escape and when he finally did, he sustained an ear injury.

THROUGHOUT his career, Mick Foley has treated the WWE Universe to some heart-stopping moments. Whether as the brutally violent Cactus Jack, unhinged Mankind, goofy Dude Love, or as himself, Mick Foley has provided some indelible memories.

6 THREE CHANCES

All three of Mick Foley's personas competed in the 1998 *Royal Rumble Match*, giving Foley three chances to win. Cactus Jack was up first, bringing trash cans to the ring, and lost to Chainsaw Charlie. Mankind was 16th, but was soon tossed from the ring. Dude Love was 28th, but he was not able to win either.

7 BETRAYED

In 2006, WWE Chairman Mr. McMahon threatened to fire Foley's ally Melina unless Foley kissed his bare backside. Loyal Foley reluctantly agreed to do it. Just seconds after Foley smooched the boss's bottom, Melina attacked Foley and he was fired instead of her.

6

9

8 DOWN A FLIGHT OF STAIRS

WWE decided to honor Mick Foley as the Hardcore Legend he was with a special ceremony at Madison Square Garden in New York. Jealous legend-killer Randy Orton saw the perfect opportunity to add to his resume by jumping Foley backstage and kicking him down a flight of stairs.

9 EMPTY ARENA

At halftime of Super Bowl XXXIII, Mankind and The Rock fought for the WWE Championship in an Empty Arena Match. To ensure no one could interfere, they competed in a building without any fans. The action spilled backstage where Mankind pinned The Rock with a forklift and a cargo pallet.

10 THE BIRTH OF MR. SOCKO

While Mr. McMahon was in the hospital recovering from an attack by Undertaker and Kane, Mankind tried to cheer him up with Mr. Socko, a sock puppet. Mankind went on to use the puppet on his opponents, sticking it down their throats in a submission move.

TOP 10
GOOD GUYS GONE BAD

THE WWE UNIVERSE IS loyal to the core, and they give their full support to their favorite Superstars. When Superstars start behaving badly, it can take years for the WWE Universe to get over the betrayal— if they ever do at all.

1 HULK HOGAN

Bad guys Scott Hall and Kevin Nash had promised a third man in their revolutionary group. When fan-favorite and former all-around good guy Hulk Hogan was revealed as the final member of the villainous trio, the fans in attendance expressed their disgust by pelting the ring with trash.

2 ANDRE THE GIANT

In 1987, both Hulk Hogan and the WWE Universe were devastated to learn that Andre the Giant had decided to align himself with underhanded manager Bobby "the Brain" Heenan. The pair planned to stop at nothing to take the WWE Championship away from Hulk Hogan.

3 THE FABULOUS FREEBIRDS

During a Steel Cage Match in Dallas, Texas in 1982, hometown hero Kerry Von Erich thought he had the support of the Freebirds team. Instead, they slammed the cage door on him, starting a rivalry between the beloved Von Erich family and the now-hated Freebirds.

4 SHAWN MICHAELS

The Rockers tag team of Shawn Michaels and Marty Jannetty appeared on Brutus Beefcake's interview show *The Barber Shop*. Michaels callously attacked his partner during the show, tossing him through a window to the disgust of the WWE Universe.

5 STONE COLD STEVE AUSTIN

For years, WWE boss Mr. McMahon and Stone Cold Steve Austin were at odds, with Austin refusing to bend to McMahon's will. But to win the WWE Championship at *WrestleMania X-Seven*, Austin teamed up with Mr. McMahon, leaving the WWE Universe in shock.

6 LARRY ZBYSZKO

Two-time WWE Champion Bruno Sammartino was aspiring Superstar Larry Zbyszko's mentor. Eventually, Zbyszko tried to prove that he was more than just a student by brutally attacking the beloved Bruno Sammartino with a chair, enraging the WWE Universe.

7 BATISTA

Batista formed an unlikely friendship with underdog, Rey Mysterio. But when Mysterio unintentionally prevented him from winning the World Heavyweight Championship in 2009, Batista shocked the WWE Universe by decimating his former tag team partner.

8 OWEN HART

Owen Hart took sibling rivalry to historic levels in 1994 when he attacked his more successful brother, Bret, out of pure jealousy. It launched a year-long rivalry that increased in intensity when Bret won the WWE Championship at *WrestleMania X*.

9 SETH ROLLINS

The WWE Universe was solidly behind the intrepid trio of Superstars in The Shield. But their impressive two-year run of success came to a screeching halt when Seth Rollins betrayed Shield-mates Dean Ambrose and Roman Reigns and joined rival stable, The Authority.

10 PAUL ORNDORFF

Paul Orndorff changed his villainous ways and teamed with Hulk Hogan to the delight of the WWE Universe. But the change did not last long as Orndorff attacked Hogan, and turned his back on the fans.

TOP 10
BAD GUYS GONE GOOD

SPORTS ENTERTAINMENT fans love to hate bad guys, and the WWE Universe never holds back in expressing disapproval through boos and chants. When villainous Superstars make a change for the better, however, boos quickly turn to cheers, and fans embrace their new hero.

1 UNDERTAKER

At first, Undertaker was an ally to baddie Jake "The Snake" Roberts in his war with Randy Savage. But when Roberts made ready to swing a chair at the lovely Miss Elizabeth, Undertaker stepped in and stopped him. The chivalrous move made him one of the WWE Universe's favorite Superstars in 1992.

2 STONE COLD STEVE AUSTIN

Many Superstars embrace the support of the WWE Universe and change their bad behavior. Austin is not one of them. But when he refused to give up at *WrestleMania 13*, continuing to the point of unconsciousness, his resilance won over fans and made him one of the most popular Superstars ever.

3 MR. PERFECT

Randy Savage needed a tag team partner for his war with Ric Flair and Razor Ramon in 1992. Flair and Ramon were furious—and the WWE Universe was thrilled—when Flair's Executive Consultant, Mr. Perfect, agreed to team with Savage.

4 KURT ANGLE

Things looked bad for the WWE in their Winner Takes All Match with the Alliance in 2001. But traitor Kurt Angle was actually a double agent and helped Team WWE win. Despite the good karma, the boastful Angle couldn't maintain his newfound popularity for long.

5 RANDY SAVAGE

At *WrestleMania VII*, Randy Savage lost a Retirement Match to Ultimate Warrior, and Savage's manager, Queen Sherri, attacked him for losing. His former manager, Miss Elizabeth, ran Sherri off before reuniting with Savage, turning a sad ending into a happy one.

6 BATISTA

Batista's fellow Evolution members, Triple H and Ric Flair, wanted Batista to challenge JBL at *WrestleMania 21*. When Batista realized that Triple H was merely protecting his own title reign, he put Triple H through a table, much to the delight of the WWE Universe.

8

7 THE SHIELD

After more than a year of inflicting their own warped brand of "justice" on WWE's heroes, the infamous trio The Shield turned their backs on the Authority in March 2014. This instantly made them popular heroes to the WWE Universe.

8 LEX LUGER

In an attempt to embarrass the U.S., WWE Champion Yokozuna challenged any American to bodyslam him on the deck of the *USS Intrepid* on Independence Day, 1993. Former bad guy Lex Luger slammed the 600-pound champion, becoming an instant fan favorite.

9 NIKITA KOLOFF

In 1986, "The Russian Nightmare," Nikita Koloff, was one of the the NWA's most loathed competitors. Stunned fans were forced to think again when the hated Koloff partnered with the beloved Dusty Rhodes in a Steel Cage Match.

1

10 TRIPLE H

Triple H and Stone Cold Steve Austin were despised as the Two Man Power Trip in 2001. However, Triple H's incredible determination to work his way back to the ring after a devastating injury won him the love of WWE fans everywhere.

RANDY ORTON

"I'M A THIRD GENERATION SUPERSTAR."

1 THE HARTS

Stu and Helen Hart had 12 children and many of them wrestled, most notably Bret and Owen. Some Superstars—Jim "The Anvil" Neidhart and the British Bulldog—joined the family through marriage. Their grandchildren, David Hart Smith and Natalya Neidhart, also competed as The Hart Dynasty.

2 THE MCMAHONS

After purchasing WWE from his father in 1982, third-generation promoter Vince McMahon transformed the regional promotion into a global empire. His children, Stephanie and Shane McMahon, have run *RAW* and *SmackDown* and held several leadership roles over the years.

3 THE ANOA'I FAMILY

The Rock is considered the most electrifying man in WWE. The Rock's father, Rocky Johnson, and grandfather, High Chief Peter Maivia, are both WWE Hall of Famers. Maivia was also a member of the Anoa'i family, which has included Rikishi, Yokozuna, the Headshrinkers, and Roman Reigns.

4 THE ORTONS

For 15 years Randy Orton has built an incredible WWE legacy that includes multiple World Championship reigns. His father, "Cowboy" Bob Orton, was a WWE fixture throughout the 1980s. Randy's grandfather, Bob Orton, Sr., also won championships in AWA and NWA.

5 THE GUERREROS

The head of the Guerrero family, Gory, was legendary in Mexico. Gory's four sons continued his legacy: Chavo, Sr. (also known as Chavo Classic in WWE), Mando, Hector, and Eddie. Eddie became a decorated Hall of Famer and also teamed with his nephew, Chavo, Jr. to form Los Guerreros.

6 THE FLAIRS

Ric Flair is the most decorated World Champion in sports entertainment history. His son David competed in WCW, and Ric's daughter, Charlotte, has held the NXT Women's Championship, the Divas Championship, and the *RAW* Women's Championship four times in her young career.

7 THE FUNKS

Sons of noted competitor and promoter Dory Funk, Terry and Dory Jr. became the first brothers to both hold the NWA World Heavyweight Championship. Dory Jr. won the Title in 1969, and Terry in 1975. He went on to pioneer the hardcore wrestling style.

8 THE HENNIGS

There have been three generations of Hennig champions. Larry "the Axe" Hennig was a Tag Team Champion in the AWA. His son, Curt, most famously known as Mr. Perfect in WWE, was an Intercontinental Champion. Curt's son, Curtis Axel, is also a former Intercontinental Champion.

9 THE STEINERS

Rick and Scott Steiner began their tag team career in WCW, but the brothers also managed to win multiple championships in both WWE and Japan. With their mix of innovative offensive maneuvers, many consider the duo one of the greatest tag teams of all time.

10 THE HARDYS

Brothers Matt and Jeff Hardy joined WWE in 1998 and their high-risk aerial moves made them fan favorites. They won the World Tag Team Championship seven times and each found success as solo performers.

FAMILY BUSINESSES ARE common all over the world, and sports entertainment is no different. There have been many sibling and multi-generational competitors— as well as some intense family disputes—which have been settled in the ring over the years.

TOP 10 TEXAN SUPERSTARS

THERE'S A SAYING THAT everything is bigger in Texas. That's definitely true in sports entertainment—the Lone Star state is home to an enormous number of Superstars. Texas's rich wrestling history has produced dozens of World Champions, several local promotions, and multiple *WrestleMania* events, too.

1 STONE COLD STEVE AUSTIN
VICTORIA, TEXAS

Perhaps the most popular Superstar in sports entertainment history, Stone Cold Steve Austin was a six-time WWE Champion. He got his "Texas Rattlesnake" nickname from his habit of striking down anyone in his way with a Stone Cold Stunner.

2 SHAWN MICHAELS
SAN ANTONIO, TEXAS

Shawn Michaels, "The Heartbreak Kid," won six different titles in WWE including four World Championships. He delighted his hometown fans by beating Sycho Sid for the WWE Championship at San Antonio's Alamodome at the 1997 *Royal Rumble*.

3 THE VON ERICH FAMILY
DENTON, TEXAS

This proud dynasty has produced three generations of championship contenders. The Von Erichs were the backbone of the Texas promotion World Class Championship Wrestling, and Kerry Von Erich once held the NWA World Heavyweight Championship.

4 TERRY FUNK & DORY FUNK JR.
AMARILLO, TEXAS

Trained by their father, Dory Funk, Terry and Dory Jr. brought a spicy Texas tang to the ring with their hard-nosed, punishing style. The pair made history by being the first brothers to both hold the prestigious NWA World Heavyweight Championship.

5 DUSTY RHODES
AUSTIN, TEXAS

Rhodes played college football at West Texas State before moving to sports entertainment, where he won three World Championships. As Dusty rose to global prominence, he shed his villain status to become the personification of the common man.

6 BOOKER T
HOUSTON, TEXAS

Few competitors from any state can boast a resume as impressive as Booker T's. During his time in WCW and WWE, Booker won no less than 13 tag team championships and an astounding 19 singles championships.

7 EDDIE GUERRERO
EL PASO, TEXAS

Perhaps the most notable of the Guerrero wrestling family, Eddie competed in both Mexico and the USA. His career reached its pinnacle at *No Way Out* 2004, when he won the WWE Championship from Brock Lesnar.

8 JBL
SWEETWATER, TEXAS

JBL first hit the scene as Bradshaw, a tough brawler who won several tag team championships as part of the APA. But after walking out on the APA, he made his mark, winning the WWE Championship in 2004 in the persona of a New York City tycoon.

9 WENDI RICHTER
DALLAS, TEXAS

A 2010 inductee into the WWE Hall of Fame, Dallas native Wendi Richter was a two-time WWE Women's Champion. One of her title victories was at the inaugural *WrestleMania*, where she defeated Leilani Kai, cheered on by pop star Cyndi Lauper.

10 TULLY BLANCHARD
SAN ANTONIO, TEXAS

Blanchard dominated San Antonio-based Southwest Championship Wrestling, winning the Heavyweight Championship six times, along with numerous NWA championships. He was a founding member of The Four Horsemen.

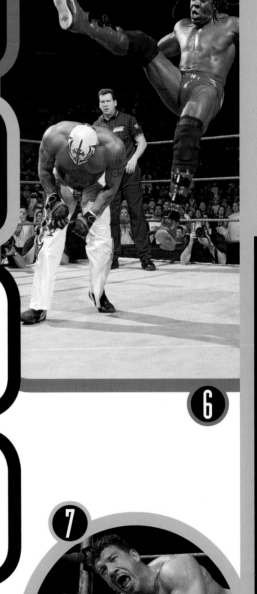

6

7

TOP 10
NXT CHAMPIONS

Since 2012, **NXT** has featured up-and-coming Superstars looking to make their name in **WWE**. The champions of **NXT** have become some of the brightest stars.

1 FINN BALOR On July 4, 2015, Irish Superstar Finn Balor beat reigning champion Kevin Owens for the NXT Championship in Japan. Balor held the title for a record-breaking nine months.

2 ADRIAN NEVILLE The most decorated NXT champion, Neville held the title for almost 10 months, and won the NXT Tag Team Championship with Oliver Grey and Corey Graves.

3 THE ASCENSION The Ascension had the longest NXT Tag Team Championship reign in the title's early history. From September 2013, they defended the title until losing it just one day shy of a year.

4 PAIGE Paige was the first Superstar to win the NXT Women's Championship and held it until she moved to *RAW*.

5 BO DALLAS In 2013, Dallas became the youngest NXT Champion at 22. Later on *RAW*, he had an impressive winning streak.

6 SAMOA JOE In November 2016 Samoa Joe became the first Superstar to ever hold the NXT Championship twice.

7 ASUKA The fifth NXT Women's Champion, Asuka won the title in April 2016, and has dominated ever since.

8 THE REVIVAL Scott Dawson and Dash Wilder, better known as The Revival, were the first team to win the NXT Tag Team Championship twice.

9 BIG E On a long winning streak, Big E pinned opponents for a five count instead of three, becoming the second NXT Champion.

10 CHARLOTTE The second Women's Champion in NXT history, Charlotte held the title for more than eight months before losing it to her rival Sasha Banks in a Fatal 4-Way Match.

"Ravishing" Rick Rude disrobes before a match.

Samoa Joe (right); Finn Balor battles Kevin Owens for the NXT Championship (above).

TOP 10
80s SUPERSTARS

Many 1980s Superstars are still loved for their huge personalities and efforts to capture the attention of the WWE Universe.

1 THE JUNKYARD DOG The Hall of Famer often brought audience members to the ring to dance to his funky entrance song, "Grab Them Cakes."

2 WENDI RICHTER Teaming up with popstar Cyndi Lauper, Richter turned fans' attention to female competitors.

3 "RAVISHING" RICK RUDE This vain Superstar demanded silence when he removed his warm-up robe in the ring.

4 KOKO B. WARE The WWE Universe flapped their arms along with Koko's faithful pet macaw and mascot, Frankie.

5 JIMMY HART Known as "The Mouth of the South," the manager barked instructions through his megaphone.

6 THE BUSHWHACKERS New Zealanders, Luke and Butch, licked the heads of each other and ringside fans.

7 BRUTUS "THE BARBER" BEEFCAKE The villainous rule-breaker cut his opponents' hair when he captured them in his powerful sleeper hold.

8 THE BROOKLYN BRAWLER The Brawler is remembered for bringing his street-fighting style into the ring.

9 THE MOONDOGS Tag teammates Rex and King intimidated opponents by gnawing on huge animal bones.

10 HILLBILLY JIM This burly Superstar backed up his boast that competitors shouldn't "go messin' with a country boy."

TOP 10 SUMMERSLAM SUPERSTARS

THE BIGGEST PARTY OF the summer, WWE's *SummerSlam* has been an August tradition since 1988. The event has featured incredible championship clashes, unique matches, and several competitors announcing their presence to the WWE Universe by winning major titles.

1 BROCK LESNAR

At *SummerSlam 2002*, Lesnar pinned The Rock to become the youngest WWE Champion in history, at just 24 years old. Over a decade later at *SummerSlam 2014*, Lesnar beat John Cena in a match so brutal that referee should have stopped it, but Lesnar continued and won the Title again.

2 ULTIMATE WARRIOR

At the first *SummerSlam* in 1988, Ultimate Warrior pinned Honky Tonk Man in about 30 seconds. It ended the longest Intercontinental Championship reign ever. Two years later at *SummerSlam*, Warrior defended the WWE Championship against "Ravishing" Rick Rude in a Steel Cage Match.

3 CM PUNK

SummerSlam's five-year stay in Los Angeles from 2009 to 2015 was kind to CM Punk. In 2009, he captured the World Heavyweight Championship from Jeff Hardy in a grueling Tables, Ladders, and Chairs Match, and two years later, he beat rival John Cena to be crowned undisputed WWE Champion.

4 DANIEL BRYAN

After being dismissed from the Nexus stable by leader Wade Barrett, Daniel Bryan gained revenge at *SummerSlam 2010* by joining WWE in their elimination victory over the Nexus. Bryan bested monstrous Kane at *SummerSlam 2012* and took the WWE Championship at *SummerSlam 2013*.

5 BRITISH BULLDOG

In 1992, the first *SummerSlam* to be held outside North America took place at Wembley Stadium in London, United Kingdom. The British Bulldog delighted his British compatriots by beating Canadian Superstar Bret "Hit Man" Hart to capture the Intercontinental Championship.

6 RANDY ORTON

On seven occasions, Randy Orton has challenged for World Championships at *SummerSlam*, and he's been successful on five. He won matches for the World Heavyweight Championship in 2004 and 2011, and took a *Money in the Bank* opportunity to win the WWE Championship in 2013.

3

7 TRIPLE H

Triple H has won some classic *SummerSlam* contests. Victory in a Ladder Match won him the Intercontinental Championship in 1998, and he outlasted five men in an Elimination Chamber Match in 2003 to retain the World Heavyweight Championship.

8 EDGE & CHRISTIAN

While both Edge and Christian competed in numerous singles matches, the duo reached their greatest *SummerSlam* heights when they won the World Tag Team Championship in the first-ever Tables, Ladders, and Chairs Match, held at *SummerSlam 2000*.

10

9 MICK FOLEY

Competing in his Mankind persona, Mick Foley made an incredible first impression at *SummerSlam*, beating the legendary Undertaker in the first Boiler Room Brawl at *SummerSlam* 1996. Three years later, he won his third WWE Championship in a Triple Threat Match versus Triple H and Stone Cold Steve Austin.

10 BETH PHOENIX

At *SummerSlam 2008*, Beth Phoenix pinned Mickie James in a Mixed Tag Team Match to win the WWE Women's Championship. Phoenix's victory also allowed her Glamarella tag team partner, Santino Marella, to become the Intercontinental Champion.

47

TOP 10

RISING SUPERSTARS

THE WWE UNIVERSE loves watching up-and-coming Superstars rise to the top. Many young competitors have moved up from the NXT ranks to the brighter lights of *RAW* and *SmackDown Live*. Here they can exhibit their energy, stamina, and moves against more experienced opponents.

1 CHARLOTTE FLAIR

As the daughter of legendary Superstar, Ric Flair, Charlotte was born with championship pedigree. She has already surpassed expectations by winning the NXT Women's Championship once in 2014, and this is in addition to her four championship reigns in WWE.

2 KEVIN OWENS

After Finn Balor was forced to vacate the WWE Universal Championship in 2016, Kevin Owens seized the opportunity of a lifetime. Already a two-time Intercontinental Champion, Owens proved himself as a main-event mainstay by becoming WWE's second Universal Champion.

3 SASHA BANKS

Former NXT Women's Champion, Sasha Banks, joined the WWE roster in 2015 where she cemented her reuptation as "The Boss" with lightning speed. She won the WWE Women's Championship three times and headlined an episode of *RAW*.

4 AMERICAN ALPHA

NCAA wrestler, Jason Jordan, and Olympic competitor, Chad Gable, combined forces in 2015 to become American Alpha, an NXT Tag Team Championship squad. They were soon drafted to *SmackDown Live*, where they proved to be competitive in their bid for the Championship.

5 BECKY LYNCH

At *Backlash 2016*, Becky Lynch overcame five other Superstars in a Six Pack Elimination Challenge, successfully eliminating opponent Carmella by submission. This made her the first competitor to win the WWE *SmackDown* Women's Championship.

6 BAYLEY

Bayley became one of NXT's brightest Superstars, winning the NXT Women's Championship in August 2015 and retaining it in a classic Iron Man Match. She has since joined *RAW* where further success surely awaits her.

7 FINN BALOR

The first NXT competitor to be selected in the 2016 WWE Draft, Finn Balor proved his worth by winning the WWE Universal Championship at *SummerSlam 2016*. It was his first appearance in a WWE pay-per-view event.

8 ALEXA BLISS

After Becky Lynch became the first WWE *SmackDown* Women's Champion in September 2016, rookie Alexa Bliss stepped up her game and emerged as a top rival for the *SmackDown* Women's Championship. This was an impressive feat so early on in her career.

9 ENZO & BIG CASS

The incredibly popular tag team of Enzo Amore and Big Cass has given hints of a bright future. It seems to be only a matter of time until the master trashtalker and the 7-foot tall giant are champions, either in a tag team or a singles competition.

10 BRAUN STROWMAN

Introduced as the fourth member of the Wyatt Family in 2015, Strowman has been called "The New Face of Destruction" and for good reason. Since breaking out on his own, nobody on *RAW* has been able to constrain this 385-pound behemoth.

4

7

1 STING

Sting's ghoulish look intimidated his opponents.

2 LUNA VACHON

Vachon's freaky vein-like face paint terrified the competition.

3 ULTIMATE WARRIOR

Ultimate Warrior painted striking masks on his face in varying bright colors that matched his high energy levels.

4 DAMIEN 666

The fiendish Superstar brought this devilish face paint to the ring.

5 DOINK

With creepy clown face paint—and behavior to match—Doink was a mystifying opponent.

6 GOLDUST

Goldust loved gold so much he covered himself in the color from head to toe, including his face.

7 THE GREAT MUTA

The Great Muta painted his face with Japanese symbols meaning "patience" and "flame" to reflect the duality of his persona.

TOP 10
FACE-PAINTED
SUPERSTARS

BY INTIMIDATING competitors, Superstars can gain an advantage in the ring, and some use fierce face paint to help give them an edge. Others use it to express their personalities or to reflect their heritage.

UMAGA 8 ▶

Umaga competed in WWE rings for three years, painting his face with traditional Samoan patterns to reflect his heritage.

▲ 10 KAMALA

Kamala's tribal-like face paint reflected his warrior-like spirit.

◀ 9 FINN BALOR

Also known as the Demon King, Finn Balor's huge painted fangs are designed to frighten his competitors.

TOP 10 RIC FLAIR RIVALS

RIC FLAIR OFTEN SAID "To be the man, you've got to beat the man." And seeing as Flair was a 16-time World Champion, his boast served as an invitation to the numerous Superstars who targeted Flair and attempted to knock him off his perch as one of the greatest Superstars of all time.

1 STING

For the span of his WCW career, Sting's path was inextricably intertwined with Ric Flair's. In 1988, newcomer Sting stood out when he wrestled Flair to a 45-minute draw at the inaugural *Clash of the Champions*. The two battled for years, often in fierce matches for the World Heavyweight Championship.

2 DUSTY RHODES

Ric Flair's first World Championship, in 1981, came at the expense of Dusty Rhodes. Rhodes then defeated Flair in 1986 for his third and final reign as NWA World Heavyweight Champion. Rhodes' long run as Champion prevented Flair from holding the title for three and a half years.

3 RICKY STEAMBOAT

Ric Flair and Ricky Steamboat were locked in a heated rivalry for the NWA World Heavyweight Championship in 1989. That same year, Steamboat won his only title against Flair, and the two competed in a series of spectacular rematches.

4 HARLEY RACE

Harley Race ended Flair's first NWA World Heavyweight Championship reign. Knowing that Flair was a contender for the Championship, Race put up a bounty, payable to anyone who put Flair out of the competition. The plan almost worked, but Flair overcame his injuries to defeat Race at *Starrcade 1983*.

5 HULK HOGAN

For years, Hulk Hogan was the top Superstar in WWE and Flair was the standard-bearer of WCW. Many speculated who would win in a dream match between the two champions. The pair finally had intense bouts for the World Heavyweight Championship in WCW between 1994 and 1999.

6 TERRY FUNK

Funk, a former NWA World Heavyweight Champion, looked set to regain the title when he challenged Flair to a match. When Flair refused, Funk attacked him. Flair recovered and got revenge by defeating Funk at *The Great American Bash 1989*. He then forced Funk into an "I Quit" match at *Clash of the Champions IX*.

7 MAGNUM TA

Flair and the infamous Four Horsemen stable had all they could handle with the charismatic Magnum TA. The Superstar defeated Horsemen member, Tully Blanchard, for the United States Championship and then pushed NWA World Heavyweight Champion, Flair, to the limit in an highly acclaimed Title battle.

8 RANDY SAVAGE

Flair and Randy Savage started their rivalry in WWE and then renewed it in WCW. Savage beat Flair for the WWE Championship at *WrestleMania VIII*, but Flair regained it six months later. Years later, the two clashed in multiple rematches for the WCW World Heavyweight Championship.

9 LEX LUGER

Lex positioned himself against Ric Flair and The Four Horsemen in a bid to become a top contender for Flair's NWA World Heavyweight Championship. Luger came tantalizingly close to beating Flair on several occasions from 1988 through 1991 but to his dismay never succeeded.

10 RODDY PIPER

"Rowdy" Roddy Piper challenged Flair for the NWA World Heavyweight Championship, but was unsuccessful. Their rivalry crossed over to WWE when Piper declared "I scare Flair" and they captained opposing squads at *Survivor Series 1991*.

⑨

TOP 10
MATCH RULES

There are many different rules in all types of sports entertainment matches.

1 PINFALL In the most common way to win a match, opponents must hold (pin) both of their competitor's shoulders on the mat for a three-count.

2 SUBMISSION An opponent must give up by tapping the ground, their competitor, or a verbal surrender.

3 KNOCKOUT When a competitor is incapacitated, they have until the referee's count of 10 to get up, or they lose the match.

4 COUNTOUT If a Superstar leaves the ring and the referee counts to 10, that Superstar is counted out.

5 FOREIGN OBJECTS Striking an opponent with a foreign object is not permitted and will lead to disqualification.

6 TEAMMATE TAG In standard tag team matches, Superstars can swap out of the ring with teammates by tagging them.

7 TABLE BREAK In a Table Match, the winning competitor is the one who drives their opponent through a table.

8 CLIMB AND RETRIEVE In Ladder Matches, the only way to win is to climb to the top of the ladder and pull down an object, such as a title or a briefcase.

9 EXIT THE CAGE In many enclosure-based encounters, such as Steel Cage Matches, the first Superstar to pin his or her opponent or exit the structure wins.

10 LAST RIDE To secure a win in a Last Ride Match, the victor must force their opponent into the back of a hearse, shut the door, and drive it out of the arena.

TOP 10
BIZARRE MOMENTS

There have been some strange moments in the ring throughout WWE's long history.

1 STONE COLD HUG Stone Cold Steve Austin embraced his rival, Mr. McMahon in the run up to *King of the Ring 2001*, but the bizarre hug appeared tense and cold.

2 "MEAN" GENE DANCES After debuting Superstar Gobbledy Gooker hatched from an egg, normally reserved announcer Gene Okerlund square danced with the turkey.

3 DEAD DIESEL When a casket was delivered to the ring, Diesel expected to find his rival Undertaker, who often enters in a casket. Instead, a Diesel lookalike was lying inside.

4 SINGING BOSS WWE boss, Mr. McMahon, sang to introduce the annual Slammy Awards show. He was accompanied by Superstars playing back up instruments.

5 IMPERSONATORS Triple H and Shawn Michaels mocked Mr. McMahon and his son Shane by dressing like them, wearing wigs, and speaking like them to the crowd.

6 MOPPY Saturn had to choose between love interest Terri and a mop named "Moppy." He chose Moppy.

7 MOPPY NO MORE But Saturn and Moppy's romance was cut short by Raven, who threw Moppy into a woodchipper.

8 PARTY CRASHER CM Punk crashed Mysterio's daughter's ninth birthday in the ring, shocking Mysterio's family.

9 RING HAVOC In June 2010, faction Nexus debuted and tore the ring apart.

10 FUNERAL FEUD Big Boss Man enraged Big Show when he crashed his father's funeral—and dragged away the coffin.

Saturn parades his girlfriend, Moppy, around the arena.

Mr. Kennedy and Undertaker in a Last Ride Match

1

1 TOMMY DREAMER

With his passion and fighting spirit, Tommy Dreamer was in many ways the heart and soul of **ECW**. He joined the organization in 1993 and stayed with the company until it folded in 2001. He won the **ECW** Championship once in the original **ECW** and once in WWE's relaunched **ECW**.

2 TAZZ

Tazz won every championship in the original ECW multiple times, including the ECW World Heavyweight Championship, Television Championship, and the World Tag Team Championship. He also created his own world title, the FTW Championship, in May 1998.

3 ROB VAN DAM

Rob Van Dam competed in ECW from 1996 until 2001. He brought an array of innovative and punishing moves to the ring, including his self-titled Van Daminator and Van Terminator. At 23 months, Rob Van Dam holds the record for the longest ECW Television Championship reign in history.

4

4 SHANE DOUGLAS

The Franchise, as Shane Douglas called himself, was four-time ECW Champion between 1993 and 1999, with two of his reigns lasting more than a year. Douglas also won the ECW Television Championship twice during his time in ECW.

5 RAVEN

Raven first joined ECW looking for revenge against his childhood rival Tommy Dreamer, but soon became a crowd favorite. The charismatic Raven also built a stable of followers, known as "Raven's Nest," who helped Raven capture the ECW Championship on January 27, 1996.

6 FRANCINE

Managing many of ECW's biggest stars over the years, Francine earned the nickname "The Queen of Extreme" due to her unwavering dedication to her clients. Her most successful partnership came from managing Shane Douglas, who twice became the ECW Champion under Francine's tutelage.

7 SABU

When Sabu came to the ring, announcer Joey Styles described the man as a "death-defying maniac." Sabu brought a reckless style into the ring, and he was the only man other than Tazz to hold the short-lived FTW Title.

8 THE SANDMAN

The Sandman held the ECW Championship five times, more than any other ECW competitor in history. Brandishing a Singapore cane as his weapon of choice, The Sandman would leave numerous welts on anyone who crossed his path.

9 THE DUDLEY BOYZ

With eight separate championship reigns between 1997 and 1999, The Dudley Boyz were one of the most successful tag teams in ECW history. Within this three-year period, half-brothers Bubba Ray and D-Von Dudley were always in the running for the Tag Team Championship.

10 JOEY STYLES

Lending his signature voice to the ECW broadcasts, announcer Joey Styles brought a distinct style to calling the extreme action and over-the-top antics of its roster. Styles would punctuate the biggest moments with his "OH MY GOD!" catchphrase.

FOR YEARS, WWE AND WCW clashed, with each looking to be at the top of the sports entertainment world. But in 1993, ECW turned the one-on-one battle into a three-way dance. With innovative match types, ECW had a profound impact on the evolution of WWE.

TOP 10 RUTHLESS SUPERSTARS

MOST SUCCESSFUL Superstars have a mean streak, but some are especially infamous for their treatment of opponents—and sometimes of officials, announcers, and backstage personnel, too. These angry Superstars seem to enjoy hurting their foes just a little bit too much!

1 ABDULLAH THE BUTCHER

Perhaps no Superstar in history deserved their nickname more than the Butcher did. Not content to rely on his prodigious brawling skills, Abdullah would illegally attack opponents with just about any object. Most famously, he used forks to inflict pain on his foes.

2 KILLER KOWALSKI

While many fans today know Kowalski as a wrestling trainer whose most notable pupil was Triple H, he was also a fierce competitor in the ring. Several of his opponents found themselves reflecting on their defeat from a hospital bed.

3 RANDY ORTON

Orton set out to make his name in WWE by injuring Hall of Fame competitors—an approach that earned him the moniker "The Legend Killer." His specialty moves included brutal, lashing punt kicks to his rivals that would often sideline them for weeks or even months.

4 SABU

No one embodied the "Extreme" in ECW more than Sabu. This silent assailant would drive opponents through tables, use chairs as a weapon, and hit moves that caused as much damage to his own body as to his foe. Scornful of pain, he patched up his own injuries mid-bout—once using glue!

5 SID

Sid so enjoyed hurting his opponents that he was dubbed Sid Vicious during his time in WCW and Sycho Sid in WWE. He finished off many opponents with his brutal Powerbomb signature move, in which he lifted them shoulder-high before slamming them to the ring on their backs.

6 THE IRON SHEIK

The Iron Sheik was a fierce, unforgiving competitor. He exulted in hurting his opponents with powerful suplexes and slams before standing astride them and finishing them off with his dreaded move, the back-bending Camel Clutch.

5

7 BROCK LESNAR

Since his return to WWE in 2012, "The Beast" Brock Lesnar has taken greater delight than ever in punishing his opponents. Cracking bones with his Kimura Lock and beating down rivals with brutal suplexes are par for the course for this merciless marauder.

8 VADER

Vader's ruthless antics in the ring have branded him as one of history's most sadistic Superstars, but he didn't stop there. He filled his resume with further heinous acts, including injuring WWE President Gorilla Monsoon purely to express his displeasure with a decision Monsoon made.

9 BRUISER BRODY

A wild, brawling competitor, Bruiser Brody took perverse pleasure in beating down his competition. Shock haired and bushy bearded, Brody employed a style so brutal that he ended up wearing out his welcome in many rings, and was forced to move around from city to city.

10 KING KONG BUNDY

The towering King Kong Bundy had no problem using his massive bulk to punish his opponents, regardless of their own size—or lack of it. Perhaps his most inglorious moment was his unconscionable attack on Little Beaver at *WrestleMania III*.

4

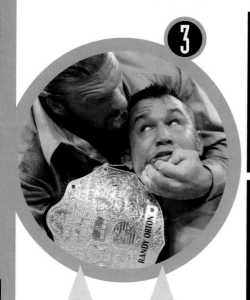

3

TRIPLE H

"YOU'LL NEVER BE A MAN."

1 SHAWN MICHAELS

Triple H's best friend and former faction mate, Shawn Michaels, returned to WWE in 2002 after a four-year hiatus. However, Triple H spoiled Shawn Michaels' emotional comeback when he knocked Michaels to the mat with his signature Pedigree, leading to a brutal Street Fight.

2 RIC FLAIR

In late 2005, Triple H teamed up with Ric Flair in a tag team match, and then betrayed his former Evolution teammate and idol with a sledgehammer attack. The two then fought in a Steel Cage Match at *Taboo Tuesday 2005* and a Last Man Standing Match at *Survivor Series 2005*.

3 RANDY ORTON

Randy Orton beat Chris Benoit to become the youngest World Heavyweight Champion at *SummerSlam 2004* at just 24 years old. But Triple H couldn't stand someone else being Champion, so he, Ric Flair, and Batista attacked Orton and kicked him out of their faction, which was known as Evolution.

4 DANIEL BRYAN

Triple H served as guest referee for Daniel Bryan's WWE Championship Match at *SummerSlam 2013* against John Cena. Following his victory, Triple H attacked Bryan, allowing Randy Orton to cash in his *Money in the Bank* briefcase to claim the WWE Championship, ending Bryan's reign after mere minutes.

4

5 D-GENERATION X

At *WrestleMania XV*, X-Pac challenged Shane McMahon for the European Championship. X-Pac thought Triple H had his back, but the powerful Superstar attacked X-Pac instead. That same night, Triple H abandoned his team, D-Generation X, to join rival group The Corporation.

6 STEPHANIE MCMAHON

Triple H even betrayed his own wife in 2002. Stephanie McMahon tried to deceive her husband when she thought he was going to leave her. Stephanie lied about being pregnant, and Triple H decided to publicly end the marriage—when they were supposed to be renewing their vows.

7 SETH ROLLINS

Seth Rollins was set to capture the new WWE Universal Championship in a Fatal 4-Way Elimination Match on *RAW* in 2016. But Triple H shocked his old protégé by faceplanting Rollins and helping Kevin Owens win the Championship.

8 BATISTA

When Batista had the opportunity to challenge Triple H for the World Heavyweight Championship at *WrestleMania 21*, Triple H tried to manipulate Batista into challenging WWE Champion JBL instead. Triple H even tried to run Batista over with a limousine identical to JBL's own.

9 MR. MCMAHON

In July 2011, Triple H tried to gain more power and get rid of WWE Chairman Mr. McMahon once and for all. Triple H stepped into the ring to deliver a message for Mr. McMahon from the Board of Directors, relieving the Chairman of his duties and leaving Triple H in charge.

10 SABLE

Triple H really didn't like to lose, and when he lost to Ultimate Warrior in his first *WrestleMania* match in 1996, he blamed his loss on his valet, Sable. Luckily, Sable's husband, Marc Mero, stepped into the ring to save his wife from Triple H's wrath.

WHILE BEING TRIPLE H'S enemy was dangerous enough, it seemed that being his ally could be even worse. When Triple H had a goal in his sights, there was no line he wouldn't cross to get it—and never a hint of remorse on his face.

TOP 10 POWER COUPLES

MANY SUPERSTARS HAVE FOUND romance in the ring, but only some have paired up with the perfect partner. By working together, Superstar couples can double their power, allowing them to dominate the competition. These powerful pairings have swept up titles and even fought for control of WWE.

Shawn Michaels and Sensational Sherri

Jimmy Uso, Naomi, and Jey Uso

1 TRIPLE H AND STEPHANIE MCMAHON

The husband and wife team has worked together to help several villainous Superstars achieve greatness, including Triple H himself.

2 RANDY SAVAGE AND MISS ELIZABETH

Savage's manager, Miss Elizabeth, helped him win multiple titles. The two then married at *SummerSlam 1991*.

3 EDGE AND VICKIE GUERRERO

Edge's manager and girlfriend, Vickie, served as *SmackDown* General Manager and helped Edge hold onto the World Heavyweight Championship.

4 GOLDUST AND MARLENA

Marlena managed her husband, Goldust, between 1996 and 1998, and twice helped him win the Intercontinental Championship.

5 BOOKER T AND SHARMELL

Sharmell often interfered in her husband, Booker T's, matches, helping him win *King of the Ring* in 2006.

6 EDDIE GUERRERO AND CHYNA

In 2000, Guerrero's love interest, Chyna, who he called "Mamacita," helped him win the European Championship.

7 SHAWN MICHAELS AND SENSATIONAL SHERRI

Veteran Sherri helped her romantic partner, Michaels, achieve his earliest success as a singles star in WWE.

8 EDGE AND LITA

This controversial pair wreaked havoc on adversaries. Lita was key in many of Edge's battles with John Cena.

9 JIMMY USO AND NAOMI

With the support of his manager and wife, Naomi, Jimmy Uso and his twin brother, Jey, won the Tag Team Title in 2014.

10 DUSTY RHODES AND SAPPHIRE

Dusty Rhodes was always accompanied by the lovely Sapphire until she betrayed him on behalf of Ted DiBiase.

TOP 10 EUROPEAN SUPERSTARS

SPORTS ENTERTAINMENT is a global phenomenon, so it's no surprise that it has attracted competitors from all over the world. Europe has produced its fair share of champions and Hall of Famers who the WWE Universe has alternately cheered and booed.

1 BRUNO SAMMARTINO
ABRUZZO, ITALY

Sammartino immigrated from Italy to the United States in the 1950s. The bodybuilder joined the world of sports entertainment in 1959, and remains the longest-reigning WWE World Champion in history.

2 ANDRE THE GIANT
GRENOBLE, FRANCE

Andre the Giant competed all over the globe from the 1970s to the 1990s. At 7-feet 4-inches tall, Andre the Giant's size made his presence in the ring unforgettable. Although he retired in 1992, he is still the Superstar that all big men are compared to.

3 BARON MIKEL SCICLUNA
ISLE OF MALTA

1996 Hall of Fame inductee Baron Mikel Scicluna was a notorious cheat, often hitting opponents with foreign objects while the official was distracted. He won both the World Tag Team Championship and United States Tag Team Championship in WWE.

4 WILLIAM REGAL
BLACKPOOL, ENGLAND

William Regal has seen incredible success both in and out of the ring. After a competitive career that saw him win more than a dozen championships, Regal went on to become an authority figure on both *RAW* and NXT.

5 NIKOLAI VOLKOFF
MOSCOW, SOVIET UNION

Whenever Volkoff competed, the WWE Universe would be subjected to his enthusiastic rendition of the Soviet national anthem. He won the World Tag Team Championship at *WrestleMania* with fellow Hall of Famer The Iron Sheik in 1985.

6 SHEAMUS
DUBLIN, IRELAND

Known as the **Celtic Warrior**, Sheamus joined **WWE** in 2006 and has become the most successful Irish Superstar in **WWE** history. Sheamus has captured four world championships, won a *Royal Rumble* match, and was the King of the Ring in 2010.

7 FIT FINLAY
BELFAST, NORTHERN IRELAND

Fit Finlay was a fierce competitor in the ring, winning championships in both WCW and WWE. Now retired, he focuses his efforts on training a new generation of Superstars, including several Women's Champions.

8 IVAN PUTSKI
KRAKOW, POLAND

Putski competed around the world for decades, regularly nailing opponents with his Polish Hammer signature move. He was inducted into the WWE Hall of Fame in 1995, and teamed with Tito Santana to win the WWE World Tag Team Championship in 1979.

9 SPIROS ARION
ATHENS, GREECE

Arion went from fan favorite to villain by hiring the hated "Classy" Freddie Blassie as his manager. In a career spanning the 1960s and 1970s, he won three United States Tag Team Championships, including one with WWE Hall of Famer Bruno Sammartino.

10 CESARO
LUCERNE, SWITZERLAND

Acknowledged as one of the strongest Superstars in WWE, Swiss Superstar Cesaro has won singles and tag team championships as well as the inaugural Andre the Giant Memorial Battle Royal at *WrestleMania 30*.

SHEAMUS

"THE WARRIOR BOWS TO NO KING."

6

TOP 10 INCREDIBLE FACTIONS

A STABLE OF SUPERSTARS can dominate in the ring. Bigger than a tag team, a faction generally contains three or more like-minded individuals who have similar goals. With numbers on their side, it is almost impossible to defeat a well-run Superstar faction.

1 THE FOUR HORSEMEN

Ric Flair, Tully Blanchard, and Arn and Ole Anderson pooled their efforts as the Four Horsemen in the mid 1980s. The members were all champions at different times, holding between them the World Heavyweight, Television, and Tag Team Championships. As the stable evolved, it continued to dominate WCW into the 90s.

2 THE NEW WORLD ORDER

When Scott Hall and Kevin Nash left WWE in 1996, they invaded rival WCW as The Outsiders. They promised a revolution was coming and shocked the world when they revealed that their third member was Hulk Hogan. The group became the nWo and would soon swell to more than 20 members.

3 D-GENERATION X

Initially formed by Triple H, Shawn Michaels, Rick Rude and Chyna, D-Generation X was a group that continually crossed lines. When X-Pac and the New Age Outlaws joined, the antics continued. The group occasionally inflicted chaos on the new generation of Superstars and terrorized Mr. McMahon.

4 THE SHIELD

Shield members, Roman Reigns, Dean Ambrose, and Seth Rollins began as a hated pack of rebels. But when they turned against The Authority faction they became instant favorites. They brought their unique brand of justice to WWE until Rollins shockingly betrayed the group in 2014.

5 THE DANGEROUS ALLIANCE

Versions of the Dangerous Alliance existed in the AWA, WCW, and ECW. The common element to all was the manager of the groups, Paul E. Dangerously, later known as Paul Heyman. The most successful version of the stable featured "Ravishing" Rick Rude and Stone Cold Steve Austin.

6 THE CORPORATE MINISTRY

In early 1999, two powerful factions, The Corporation, led by Shane McMahon, and Undertaker's Ministry of Darkness, loomed over WWE. The groups merged into The Corporate Ministry, leaving brave Superstars such as Stone Cold Steve Austin and The Rock to resist their evil agenda.

7

7 THE NEXUS

The first season of NXT featured eight rookies competing for a WWE contract. Wade Barrett won; however, the group decided to wreak havoc until they all received contracts. Named The Nexus, they carried out heinous attacks on the likes of John Cena and Mr. McMahon, proving no one was safe.

THE SHIELD

"WE'RE A SHIELD FROM INJUSTICE."

4

8 EVOLUTION

In early 2003, World Heavyweight Champion Triple H formed a faction with members that were meant to represent the evolution of sports entertainment. Featuring the legendary Ric Flair and young stars Batista and Randy Orton, the group kept a stranglehold over *RAW*.

9 THE ALLIANCE

WWE owner Vince McMahon thought he'd purchased WCW. However, his son, Shane, had bought the rival company. Shane combined his new Superstars with those of ECW, which had been purchased by his sister Stephanie. The two then invaded WWE in an attempt to put their father out of business.

10 THE BLUE WORLD ORDER

ECW's parody of the New World Order featured Superstars Stevie Richards, Hollywood Nova, and The Blue Meanie. The bWo wore trademark blue shirts and was an ECW mainstay from 1996 to 1998.

TOP 10 INTERVIEW SHOWS

SOME OF THE MOST memorable exchanges in sports entertainment history have taken place on interview shows hosted by WWE Superstars. A cast of big personalities guaranteed that these interview segments would lead to both verbal and physical altercations.

1 PIPER'S PIT

In the 1980s, some of the most significant and controversial moments in WWE history took place on *Piper's Pit*. One memorable episode featured a confrontation between Hulk Hogan and Andre the Giant, setting the stage for their *WrestleMania III* WWE Championship Match.

2 HIGHLIGHT REEL

The *Highlight Reel* debuted in 2003. With the lavishly expensive plasma screen TV, the Jeritron 5000, looming over the mat, the elite of WWE typically endured insults from host Chris Jericho. Interviews often turned into physical altercations provoked by Jericho or by his guests.

3 THE BROTHER LOVE SHOW

Brother Love got under the skin of the WWE Universe. His interview program often spelled trouble for the heroes of WWE, including Hulk Hogan and Jake "The Snake" Roberts—Superstars often found themselves blindsided by rivals!

4 BARBER SHOP

After an injury, Brutus "the Barber" Beefcake hosted the *Barber Shop* interview segment from 1991 to 1992. The show was imprinted on the memory of the WWE Universe after Shawn Michaels tossed his tag team partner, Marty Jannetty, through the Barber Shop's window!

5 FLAIR FOR THE GOLD

16-time World Champion Ric Flair briefly hosted a talk show in which he interviewed former and future rivals. In 1993, Flair introduced a new mystery man, The Shockmaster, who made a memorable debut when he crashed through a wall of the set.

6 THE CUTTING EDGE

In late 2005, Edge and his girlfriend Lita were the most hated couple in WWE. They antagonized the WWE Universe further by creating Edge's own talk show, *Cutting Edge*. The show often crossed personal lines to annoy rivals such as Ric Flair and John Cena.

6

7 FUNERAL PARLOR

After debuting as Undertaker's manager, Paul Bearer began hosting *Funeral Parlor*. The eerie atmosphere helped Paul Bearer and Undertaker intimidate a number of Undertaker's rivals, particularly Hulk Hogan and Jake Roberts.

8 ROGERS' CORNER

One of the first-ever regular WWE talk-show segments was hosted by WWE's inaugural World Champion, Buddy Rogers. In the segment, Rogers asked hard-hitting questions of legends, including future Hall of Famers Bob Backlund and Jimmy "Superfly" Snuka.

9 THE DIRT SHEET

WWE Tag Team Champions John Morrison and The Miz created an online show called *The Dirt Sheet*. While they would occasionally interview other Superstars, many episodes featured them mocking competitors, including Finlay and D-Generation X.

10 THE FLOWER SHOP

After "Rowdy" Roddy Piper left WWE, his rival Adrian Adonis created an interview segment, which often featured Piper's former allies Paul Orndorff and "Cowboy" Bob Orton. When Piper returned, he destroyed the set of *The Flower Shop*.

7

TOP 10
SUPERSTAR T-SHIRTS

MANY SUPERSTARS WEAR a signature T-shirt that reflects their specific mindset or style. The message or image on a Superstar's top can also act as a warning to competitors, or as a reminder to the WWE Universe about a Superstar's greatness.

1 AUSTIN 3:16

Austin poked fun at his religious opponent, Jake "The Snake" Roberts by renaming a well-known Psalm after himself, using some colorful language in the process. Following this, Austin wore a T-shirt with a reminder of his cutting verbal slam.

2 NWO

At *Bash at the Beach 1996*, fans pelted the ring with garbage when the legendary Hulk Hogan joined outsiders Scott Hall and Kevin Nash in the unsanctioned faction, New World Order. The street-gang style group, who wanted to take over WCW, wore T-shirts with the NWO logo (styled nWo) on them, as a reminder of their intention rule the company.

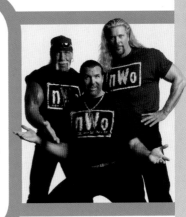

3 MACHO MAN

In the late 1980s, "Macho Man" Randy Savage sported a new eye-catching purple T-shirt. The simple, yet colorful shirt boasted Randy Savage's nickname: Macho Man. It also featured the pair of signature sunglasses he wore when entering the ring in over-the-top, often glitzy outfits.

4 HOT ROD

"Rowdy" Roddy Piper, the quintessential bad guy and the entertaining host of the *Piper's Pit* interview show, was also known as "Hot Rod." He often wore a white T-shirt printed with the phrase, which represented his hot temper, stylized as raging yellow and red flames.

5 8-BIT SHIRT

John Cena has worn an incredible array of T-shirts throughout his career, but none were as innovative as his 8-bit videogame shirt. Cena's shirt paid homage to old-school wrestling video games, showing a pixelated version of Cena on the front and the controller buttons needed to hit his 5-Knuckle Shuffle move on the back.

CONTINUED

6 EAT, SLEEP, CONQUER, REPEAT

When Brock Lesnar returned to WWE after conquering the world of mixed martial arts in UFC (Ultimate Fighting Championship), he was on a mission to take down anyone who challenged him. Lesnar's advocate, Paul Heyman, put it best by saying that Lesnar was looking to "eat, sleep, conquer, repeat." The slogan soon appeared on a T-shirt as a warning to Lesnar's challengers.

7 RED HANDPRINT

Andre the Giant was a massive man, weighing more than 500 pounds. A T-shirt with his actual-size handprint on the front and footprint on the back reminded anyone who might think about crossing the 7-foot 4-inch Superstar of his huge size.

8 WANTED DEAD

Mick Foley's Cactus Jack T-shirt showed an old-style western "Wanted Dead" poster with his own portrait on it above the words: "The World's Most Dangerous Wrestler." With this shirt, Cactus Jack warned competitors of his maniacal behavior in the ring.

9 HULKAMANIA

Hulk Hogan's signature yellow and red T-shirt was perhaps most famous for the way Hogan ripped it off his body prior to his matches. Whether in tact or torn down the middle, the term "Hulkamania" splayed across the chest was an iconic symbol of Hogan's popularity during the 1980s.

10 D-GENERATION X

An anti-establishment group, D-Generation X were known for their rebellious antics and crude behavior. Their first T-shirt had a simple but effective design of an X on the front with "D-Generation" printed over it.

D-Generation X members, Triple H and Shawn Michaels.

TOP 10 WWE HOLLYWOOD PERFORMERS

CHARISMA IS NOT CONFINED to the ring. No wonder, then, that so many of WWE's most watchable Superstars—past and present—have made a successful transition to the silver screen, scoring hits in films of all genres as well as TV shows. Here are 10 WWE Superstars who have made as big an impact in Hollywood as they have in the sports entertainment arena.

Cena is a discharged marine who clashes with a dangerous gang in the *The Marine*.

The Rock plays an Akkadian warrior named Mathayus in *The Scorpion King*.

1 THE ROCK

The Rock has rocked Hollywood in the *Fast & Furious* and *G.I. Joe* franchises, as well as comedies and action films.

2 BATISTA

"The Animal" seemed born to play sinister characters, such as Mr. Hinx in the James Bond film *Spectre*.

3 JOHN CENA

The star of WWE movies *The Marine* and *12 Rounds*, Cena proved he was a fine comedian, too, in the film *Trainwreck*.

4 THE MIZ

The Miz has starred in the third, fourth, and fifth editions of *The Marine,* as well as two holiday films.

5 HULK HOGAN

Hogan blazed a trail, becoming the first WWE Superstar to take on Hollywood when he debuted in 1982's *Rocky III*.

6 TRIPLE H

As well as acting in film and on TV, Triple H has provided voiceovers in two Scooby-Doo films and a *Surf's Up* sequel.

7 BIG SHOW

Big Show played Captain Insano in *The Waterboy*, a giant Santa in *Jingle All the Way*, and Walter Krunk in *Knucklehead*.

8 THE GREAT KHALI

India's first WWE Superstar, Khali played a number of roles including musclebound villain Dalip in *Get Smart*.

9 EDGE

After a career-ending injury, Edge took his talents to the screen, becoming a regular on the TV series *Haven*.

10 LANA

Rusev's wife and manager, Lana, took on her biggest role to date when she co-starred with Edge in *Interrogation*.

TOP 10 WWE THINGS WE MISS

THE WORLD OF SPORTS entertainment is always changing. Sometimes that means the WWE Universe has to say goodbye to well-known institutions to make room for exciting innovations. Many fans still look back fondly at those legendary events of the past.

1. THE 24/7 RULE
2000–2002

When Crash Holly first won the WWE Hardcore Championship in 2000, he boasted that he could defend it at any time. This led to the 24/7 Rule, stating that the Hardcore Champion could be pinned at any time—as long as there was a referee present! Eric Bischoff dissolved the rule in 2002.

2. TELEVISION TITLES
1974–2000

The WCW World Television Championship and the ECW World Television Championship were defended on weekly television programs with matches that had strict time limits. The titles contained fevered action and those who won often became World Champions later in their careers.

3. BODYGUARDS
1980s–2000s

Some competitors decided to tilt their in-ring encounters in their favor by employing bodyguards to watch their backs—in and out of the ring. These massive individuals often had no problem breaking the rules for their employers when the official was distracted.

4. SHOWDOWNS AT SHEA
1972–1980

Between 1972 and 1980, three WWE summer supercards were held in the home of the New York Mets baseball team: Shea Stadium, which was demolished in 2009. Fans had the chance to experience incredible matches in the unique environment of an outdoor stadium.

5. CAREER UNDERDOGS
1970s–1990s

From the 70s to the 90s, men and women tried to make a name for themselves battling the top Superstars. These overmatched competitors hoped to seize their own stunning victory in the ring. Some, like Iron Mike Sharpe, Pez Whatley, and Barry Horowitz even developed cult followings.

6 HALLOWEEN HAVOC

1989–2000

For 12 years, fans enjoyed *Halloween Havoc*, which provided a classic stage complete with a giant jack-o-lantern. The annual event gave rise to "Spin the Wheel, Make the Deal," in which a match's conditions were determined by a huge wheel. This concept evolved into WWE's *RAW Roulette*.

6

7 ANIMAL COMPANIONS

1980s–1990s

Many Superstars in the 1980s brought pets to the ring to gain a competitive advantage. Their pets could be a distraction, like Koko B. Ware's beloved bird Frankie, or a source of fear, like Jake "The Snake" Roberts' pythons, Damien and Lucifer.

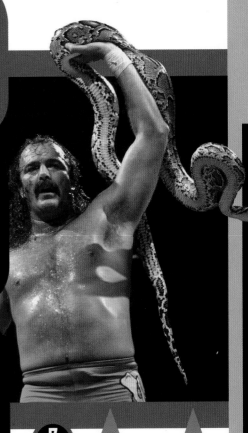

8 SIX-MAN TAG TEAM TITLES

1970s–1991

Most tag teams today are duos, but in the 1970s, 1980s, and in 1991, the National Wrestling Alliance (NWA) awarded trios with the Six-Man Tag Team Championship. The most famous team to hold the Championships were the tag team The Road Warriors (Hawk and Animal) and Dusty Rhodes.

9 WARGAMES

1987–2000

In *WarGames*, teams of four or five competed in a double-ring, which was then enclosed in a huge steel cage. One competitor would start for each side and then Superstars would enter one at a time at set intervals. This meant one team would consistently have a one-man advantage in the brutal bouts.

7

JAKE ROBERTS

"THE SNAKE WILL ALWAYS BITE BACK."

10 BLUE BARS

1986–1997

To date, Steel Cage Matches have mainly been held inside chain-link cages, which prevent outside interference. However, the Hogan vs. Bundy WWE title match at *WrestleMania 2* was held in a blue-barred cage, setting the standard for the next 10 years.

TOP 10
UNEXPECTED BREAKUPS

Sometimes ego and jealousy get in the way and former friends, tag team partners, and relatives become bitter rivals.

1 THE ROCKERS Shawn Michaels was ready to go solo in 1992, so he tossed his partner Marty Jannetty through a window.

2 THE MEGAPOWERS Jealousy and bitterness caused a rift between Hulk Hogan and Randy Savage. They fought against each other for the WWE World Heavyweight title at *WrestleMania V*, and Hogan was victorious.

3 THE STEINER BROTHERS After a decade together, Scott Steiner attacked his brother Rick in 1998 and joined the New World Order.

4 THE BELLAS At *SummerSlam 2014*, Brie Bella faced Stephanie McMahon but lost when her twin and partner Nikki betrayed her.

5 THE HARDYS When Jeff Hardy was offered a shot at the Intercontinental Championship in 2002, his brother Matt's envy overwhelmed him, and he attacked Jeff.

6 MIZ & MORRISON When Morrison accidentally made The Miz lose a 2009 match, The Miz attacked him out of spite.

7 STRIKE FORCE Tito Santana accidentally knocked into his partner Rick Martel, so Martel left him in the ring.

8 EDGE & CHRISTIAN When Edge won the 2001 *King of the Ring* Title, partner Christian was jealous and attacked him.

9 THE ROCK 'N' SOCK CONNECTION In 1999, Mankind found a book he had given The Rock, his tag team partner, in the trash. Mistakenly believing The Rock had thrown it out, Mankind started a bitter rivalry.

10 CODY RHODES & HARDCORE HOLLY Cody Rhodes was already a World Tag Team Champion with Hardcore Holly, but he betrayed Holly at the Night of Champions to take the title with new partner, Ted DiBiase.

TOP 10
UNEXPECTED REUNIONS

Although teams often split, they occasionally get back together to the great excitement of the WWE Universe.

1 RANDY SAVAGE & MISS ELIZABETH After a public split, Savage and Elizabeth made up when he lost his Retirement Match at *WrestleMania VII* to The Ultimate Warrior.

2 ROCK 'N' SOCK CONNECTION At *WrestleMania XX*, Mick Foley needed a partner to face Evolution, so he recruited The Rock, and reformed the Rock 'n' Sock Connection.

3 EVOLUTION In 2014, with The Shield as common enemy, Triple H, Batista, and Randy Orton revived Evolution.

4 NEW AGE OUTLAWS After 12 years apart, New Age Outlaws returned in July 2012 to win an incredible sixth WWE Tag Team Championship.

5 EDGE & CHRISTIAN In 2011, Edge and Christian reunited to fight Alberto Del Rio and Brodus Clay.

6 THE ROCKERS After a brutal breakup, the Rockers reformed to take on La Resistance in 2005.

7 NEW WORLD ORDER (NWO) With their rebellious attitudes, nWo changed sports entertainment, and treated fans to an unforgettable reunion during *WrestleMania 31*.

8 THE BELLAS After Nikki's betrayal at *SummerSlam 2014*, the twins reconciled and joined forces again in the ring.

9 D-GENERATION X Shawn Michaels and Triple H had been rivals for years but reformed D-Generation X in 2006.

10 THE HARDYS After their split in 2002, Matt and Jeff Hardy reformed their successful partnership in 2006, and soon won the World Tag Team Championship.

Randy Savage and Miss Elizabeth, reunited.

The Bellas (left); The Rockers (above)

IN THE RING

TOP 10s

John Cena, Seth Rollins, and Brock
Lesnar at *Royal Rumble 2015*

⑤

①

1 SANTINO MARELLA

In 2007, WWE Chairman Mr. McMahon chose a fan named **Santino Marella** from the crowd in Milan, Italy, to face the monstrous Umaga for the Intercontinental Championship. Marella seemed destined for a pummelling, but he stunned the world by winning the Title in his debut match.

2 CHRIS JERICHO

In 1999, the WWE had a clock for the countdown to the Millennium, but the clock stopped suddenly on an episode of *RAW* on August 9th. When the countdown reached zero, out strutted debut Superstar Chris Jericho, who immediately—but not wisely—picked a fight with The Rock.

3 GAIL KIM

A true baptism of fire, Gail Kim's debut in 2003 saw her take on six other female Superstars in a Battle Royal Match. Far from being daunted, Kim outlasted all her fellow competitors to win the match and the vacant Women's Championship—a title she would hold for a month.

4 THE SHIELD

Dean Ambrose, Roman Reigns, and Seth Rollins first stormed the WWE ring as a trio in 2012 during a Triple Threat Match for the WWE Championship. They delivered a Triple Powerbomb to Ryback, lifting him to their shoulders before slamming him on his back, enabling CM Punk to retain his title.

5 FANDANGO

The arrogant Fandango was supposed to have his debut match on *SmackDown*, but he kept putting it off because he didn't like people mispronouncing his name. Fandango ended up competing in his first match on the grand stage of *WrestleMania 29*, where he defeated Chris Jericho.

TOP 10 DAZZLING DEBUTS

6 KEVIN OWENS

Kevin Owens' first appearance on a WWE show and his first match were both successful—at the expense of veteran Superstar John Cena. After attacking and flooring Cena on an episode of *RAW* in 2015, Owens went on to triumph in his debut match against the Superstar a few weeks later.

7 MNM

Tag team MNM (Mercury, Nitro, and Melina) faced a challenging debut in 2005 when they competed against WWE Tag Team Champions Rey Mysterio and Eddie Guerrero for the Title. MNM beat the champions, and held the Title for more than three months.

8 THE ROCK

As a third-generation Superstar, The Rock had both a championship pedigree and a lot to live up to. Using the name Rocky Maivia, he competed in a WWE ring for the first time at *Survivor Series 1996*, where he proved his mettle by lasting the entirety of an Eight-Man Elimination Tag Team Match.

9 GOLDBERG

Goldberg's WCW streak did not get off to an especially memorable start with a win over frequent loser Hugh Morrus, but he made a bigger splash in his WWE debut. He attacked The Rock the night after *WrestleMania XIX* and then went on to pin the Superstar again in his first WWE match at *Backlash*.

10 PAIGE

The *RAW* that takes place the night after *WrestleMania* is always electric, setting the scene for the coming year. In 2014, Paige seemed to soak up the energy in the arena, stunning Divas Champion AJ Lee, and taking the Title in her first ever WWE match.

IT'S IMPORTANT TO always make a good first impression, and some rookie Superstars have really taken this advice to heart. They've come roaring in, dominating the competition from the get-go, and leaving the WWE Universe wondering what dizzying heights they might one day reach.

TOP 10 ENTRANCE MUSIC

EVERY SUPERSTAR DESERVES A BIG entrance, and dramatic music really sets the scene. Superstars choose their own signature song, which plays when they enter the arena. These catchy songs excite the WWE Universe and pump up the Superstars who are entering the arena.

Bray Wyatt holds his lantern as he enters the the ring

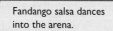

Fandango salsa dances into the arena.

1 "I WON'T DO WHAT YOU TELL ME" STONE COLD STEVE AUSTIN

The sound of breaking glass signals the entrance of Stone Cold Steve Austin into the arena.

2 "REAL AMERICAN" HULK HOGAN

The iconic Hulk Hogan's entrance music announced his dedication to fighting for the rights of all people.

3 "GRAVEYARD SYMPHONY" UNDERTAKER

While Undertaker has had many different entrance songs, the "Graveyard Symphony" is the most haunting.

4 "WHO I AM" CHYNA

The legendary Chyna's entrance song clearly affirmed that she should not be judged for being a woman, but for what she achieved in the ring.

5 "UNSTABLE" ULTIMATE WARRIOR

The driving beat of "Unstable" pumped up Ultimate Warrior and his fans as he sprinted toward the ring.

6 "METALINGUS" EDGE

When Edge entered the ring in persuit or defense of his 11 world championships, this hard rock song blared out across the arena.

7 "BURN IN MY LIGHT" RANDY ORTON

This rock anthem by Mercy Drive captured the intensity that Orton brings to the ring for every match.

8 "TURN IT UP" BAYLEY

Bayley's fun, upbeat entrance music encourages everyone around the world to turn up the music and celebrate.

9 "CHACHALALA" FANDANGO

With his salsa entrance music playing, Fandango often dances into the arena to face his opponent.

10 "LIVE IN FEAR" BRAY WYATT

The spooky sounds of "Live in Fear" fit the lantern-bearing Wyatt well.

1 JAKE ROBERTS' SNAKE

As well as besting the cunning Roberts, competitors also had to dodge Damien—the python Jake carried in his trademark sack.

2 TRIPLE H'S SLEDGEHAMMER

Triple H chose a trusty sledgehammer, often hidden under the ring, to strike fear in his opponents during matches.

3 UNDERTAKER'S URN

Initially considered by many to be the source of Undertaker's power, Undertaker would occasionally use his urn to strike adversaries.

4 JIM CORNETTE'S TENNIS RACKET

Manager Cornette waved his racket while urging on his charges. He also used it to rattle a few unsuspecting competitors!

5 XAVIER WOODS' TROMBONE

Xavier Woods carries a trombone that he uses to energize his New Day teammates and to annoy the competition.

6 MR. FUJI'S CEREMONIAL SALT

Initially brought to the ring for cleansing rituals, Mr. Fuji instead tossed the salt into Superstars' eyes to help his clients to win.

7 AL SNOW'S HEAD

Al Snow carried the head of a mannequin, named "Head," with him. The unhinged Superstar would speak to it during matches.

TOP 10
ULTIMATE RING
ACCESSORIES

MANY SUPERSTARS WILL take any shortcut to victory, even if it means breaking the rules. While some use anything they can get their hands on, other Superstars bring their own signature weapons to the ring.

◄ **8** **PAUL E. DANGEROUSLY'S PHONE**

Dangerously took his phone to his clients' matches. But he slammed it into unsuspecting opponents more often than actually taking calls.

OWEN HART'S SLAMMY AWARDS **9** ►

Hart demanded to be introduced as "Two-time Slammy Award winner Owen Hart" and brought both trophies to the ring.

▲ **THE HONKY TONK MAN'S GUITAR** **10**

The Honky Tonk Man aimed to delight fans with his guitar playing, but often simply broke the guitar over an adversary's body instead.

TOP 10

WRESTLEMANIA MAIN EVENTS

IT'S AN ACHIEVEMENT for a Superstar to compete in any *WrestleMania* match, but the ultimate honor is to be part of the last match of the evening: the main event. It's the most anticipated contest in WWE, and often, the biggest Title—the WWE Championship—is on the line.

1 · 3.29.1987

HULK HOGAN VS. ANDRE THE GIANT WRESTLEMANIA III

Hulk Hogan shocked the WWE Universe and his 500-pound challenger Andre the Giant with his remarkable strength when he slammed his massive opponent to the mat. Hogan defended the WWE Championship and dealt Andre his first defeat.

2 · 4.1.2001

THE ROCK VS. STONE COLD STEVE AUSTIN WRESTLEMANIA X-SEVEN

To defeat The Rock and win his fifth WWE Championship, Stone Cold Steve Austin did the unthinkable—he aligned himself with longtime nemesis and WWE Chairman Mr. McMahon. The unlikely pair joined forces to defeat The Rock.

3 · 3.28.2010

UNDERTAKER VS. SHAWN MICHAELS WRESTLEMANIA XXVI

After failing to end Undertaker's 16-win *WrestleMania* streak the year before, Shawn Michaels put his career on the line to convince Undertaker to grant him a rematch. In 24 minutes, Undertaker ended Michaels' 25-year career.

4 · 3.31.1985

HULK HOGAN & MR. T VS. PIPER & ORNDORFF WRESTLEMANIA I

WrestleMania became a global phenomenon when Hulk Hogan and actor Mr. T defeated "Rowdy" Roddy Piper and Paul Orndorff to conclude the first-ever edition of the "Show of Shows."

5 · 4.1.1990

HULK HOGAN VS. ULTIMATE WARRIOR WRESTLEMANIA VI

This battle between two fan favorites saw the then Intercontinental Champion Ultimate Warrior face WWE Champion Hulk Hogan. When the Warrior avoided Hogan's leg drop, he saw an opportunity to defeat him and capture his only WWE Championship.

6 — RANDY ORTON VS. BATISTA VS. BRYAN WRESTLEMANIA 30

Despite having to compete earlier the same night, Daniel Bryan took out a meddling Triple H, and overcame both Randy Orton and Batista to reach the pinnacle of his career: the WWE Championship.

10

7 — TRIPLE H VS. THE ROCK VS. BIG SHOW VS. FOLEY
WRESTLEMANIA 2000

A McMahon family member assisted each Superstar in this Fatal 4-Way Elimination Match. With help from Stephanie and Mr. McMahon, Triple H retained his WWE Title.

8 — TRIPLE H VS. JERICHO
WRESTLEMANIA X8

Overcoming a devastating leg injury, which almost ended his career in May 2001, Triple H made an astounding comeback. The Superstar known as "The Game" defeated Chris Jericho to become the second Undisputed Champion in WWE history.

1

9 — YOKOZUNA VS. BRET HART
WRESTLEMANIA X

A year after losing the WWE Championship to Yokozuna, Bret "Hit Man" Hart was able to recapture the Title, which he had lost the previous year, from the massive Superstar. Hart pinned Yokozuna and won his second WWE Championship.

10 — JOHN CENA VS. THE ROCK
WRESTLEMANIA XXVIII

In a long-anticipated "Once in a Lifetime" clash, John Cena got The Rock on the mat and tried to mock him by using his People's Elbow against him. The Rock sprung up just in time to hit a Rock Bottom, defeating Cena.

TOP 10
JAW-DROPPING
MOMENTS

A HISTORY AS RICH AND legendary as that of sports entertainment is bound to be crammed with amazing moments and controversial events. While everyone can make a list of their own personal preferences, some moments are obvious standouts. That's usually down to the sheer audacity of the characters involved in them.

1 THE MONTREAL SCREWJOB

The most infamous moment in the history of sports entertainment—which saw the birth of Mr. McMahon, evil owner of WWE—took place at *Survivor Series 1997*. Bret Hart, the current WWE Champion, was set to leave WWE. Mr. McMahon did not want him to leave with the Title. His behind-the-scenes plotting resulted in the official untruthfully claiming that Hart tapped out of a submission move.

2 THE DOUBLE REFEREES

In 1987, Ted DiBiase had tried to buy the WWE World Championship from Hulk Hogan, who refused. Hogan later faced Andre the Giant in a Title match supposedly officiated by Dave Hebner. In fact, DiBiase had paid a double (Dave's brother Earl) to take his place. Earl made a quick count to allow the Giant to win—who promptly handed the Title to DiBiase.

3 THE EXPLODING LIMO

In June 2007, Mr. McMahon appeared despondent at an episode of *RAW*. It was billed as his "appreciation night," but he was heavily booed. After a long walk of shame to the exit, he shut the door of his limo and it exploded, apparently killing him. A week later, he revealed he had faked his demise.

4 AA OF TWO SUPERSTARS

At *WrestleMania 25*, John Cena performed an amazing feat of strength when he faced Big Show and Edge in the ring. Incredibly, he hoisted both his opponents up on his back for an Attitude Adjustment. Cena rode the momentum of the astonishing move to win the World Heavyweight Championship that evening.

5 MAE YOUNG THROUGH A TABLE

The Dudley Boyz could always get the WWE Universe out of their seats by smashing an opponent through a table. But many felt the duo went a little too far on consecutive weeks of *RAW* in March 2000, when they put 77-year-old Mae Young through tables not once but twice. Young found herself propelled first off the top rope, and a week later off a stage.

CONTINUED

6 GOLDBERG WINS THE TITLE

With rookie Superstar Goldberg continuing to add victims to his impressive 1997–98 winning streak, it was only a matter of time until he got a shot at the WCW Title. Champion Hulk Hogan and his New World Order cronies tried to stack the deck against Goldberg by forcing him to battle Scott Hall first in order to earn his Title match later that night. They failed. Goldberg beat Hall, then, in front of a capacity crowd at the Georgia Dome, crushed Hulk Hogan and ushered in a new era in WCW.

7 THE COLLAPSING RING

If a competitor gets Big Show up on the top turnbuckle, they might be wise to leave him up there. In one of the greatest moments in *SmackDown* history, Brock Lesnar destroyed a ring in 2003 by superplexing Show. The throw involves lifting the opponent and falling backwards to slam him back him to the ring—in this case with disastrous results.

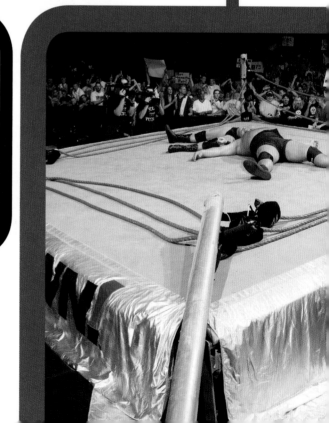

8 LAUNCHING MYSTERIO

The New World Order ran roughshod over WCW, launching attacks on its stars in and out of the ring. One of the most heinous attacks happened outside the arena in July 1996. While a match took place in the ring, Kevin Nash stalked Rey Mysterio backstage. Nash picked up Mysterio, who was about half his size, and launched him headfirst into the side of a truck.

9 LEX LUGER ON NITRO

RAW was, at one time, the only sports entertainment program on Monday nights. Then, WCW launched a competitive show, *Monday Nitro*, on September 4, 1995. The world quickly learned that WCW was a force to be reckoned with when Lex Luger appeared on the first episode, despite having been on the WWE roster for years and competing at a WWE event the night before.

10 CHYNA KEEPS HOUSE

Intercontinental Champion Jeff Jarrett was incensed that Chyna was the prime contender for his title. Jarrett held the outdated view that a woman's place was at home, not in the ring. He tried to prove the point by facing her in a Good Housekeeping Match. But Chyna struck a blow for women everywhere when she defeated Jarrett to become the first female Intercontinental Champion in history.

TOP 10
ANNOUNCERS

Sports entertainment announcers play a vital role in bringing the action to life. Whether veterans of the ring or career announcers, these personalities heighten the excitement before, during, and after a match.

1 JIM ROSS "Good ol' JR," as he is known, has been announcing sports entertainment matches for more than 35 years.

2 GORDON SOLIE An announcer for 35 years, many commentators have mimicked his precise, serious style.

3 BOBBY "THE BRAIN" HEENAN After decades as a manager, Heenan popularly moved to the broadcast booth in 1986.

4 "MEAN GENE" OKERLUND Gene joined WWE in 1984 and was famed for his interviews with top Superstars such as Hulk Hogan and The Iron Sheik.

5 JERRY "THE KING" LAWLER A former Superstar, Lawler became an announcer in 1993 and is known for his sharp one-liners and affinity for ladies.

6 MICHAEL COLE For 20 years, Cole has been calling some of the biggest matches on *Monday Night RAW* and *SmackDown*.

7 GORILLA MONSOON Gorilla Monsoon served as a commentator for more than a decade in the 1980s and 1990s, most notably paired with Jesse Ventura and Bobby Heenan.

8 JOEY STYLES Styles is famous for his catchphrase "Oh my God" which always ratchets up the excitement.

9 HOWARD FINKEL WWE legend Howard Finkel was the primary ring announcer from 1976 through to 2000.

10 LILIAN GARCIA While she is primarily a ring announcer, Garcia also sings "The Star-Spangled Banner" at some events.

Bobby "The Brain" Heenan in his announcer's chair.

TOP 10
SPORTS ENTERTAINMENT VENUES

Across the world, many arenas, stadiums, and halls have hosted big live events that have delighted the WWE Universe.

1 MADISON SQUARE GARDEN [New York, New York] This legendary venue has hosted hundreds of WWE events.

2 ECW ARENA [Philadelphia, PA] From 1993 to 2001, many of ECW's weekly television matches were taped here.

3 THE OMNI [Atlanta, Georgia] WCW held many events here, including *The Great American Bash* in 1987.

4 THE TOKYO DOME [Tokyo, Japan] In 1991, WWE partnered with Japan's Super World of Sports to hold *WrestleFest*.

5 THE 02 ARENA [London, UK] The WWE Universe in London gets rowdy at this 20,000 capacity arena.

6 THE STAPLES CENTER [Los Angeles, CA] From 2009–2014, this venue was home to *SummerSlam*. It also hosted *WrestleMania 21* in 2005.

7 AT&T STADIUM [ARLINGTON, Texas] This Texas venue hosted *WrestleMania 32* with more than 100,000 attendees.

8 SHEA STADIUM [Queens, New York] The former home of the New York Mets hosted three major WWE events in 1972, 1976, and 1980.

9 ROSEMONT HORIZON/ALLSTATE ARENA [Chicago, IL] Chicago's Allstate Arena has hosted several crucial WWE events, including three *WrestleManias*.

10 FULL SAIL LIVE [Winter Park, Florida] The next generation of WWE Superstars (NXT) competes here weekly.

The 02 Arena, London, United Kingdom

TOP 10 BRUTAL BETRAYALS

STONE COLD STEVE Austin had a famous saying: "Don't Trust Anybody." It's a motto that more Superstars would do well to adopt. Sadly, the history of sports entertainment is littered with gut-wrenching betrayals, treacherous turnabouts, and the brutal backstabbing of allies.

1 THE THIRD MAN

In 1996 the Outsiders, Scott Hall and Kevin Nash, revealed a third member of their cabal in a Tag Team Match against WCW loyalists. To everyone's shock, it was Hulk Hogan—one of WCW's biggest stars. Hogan's monumental betrayal of WCW led to the formation of the New World Order.

2 THE CORPORATE CHAMPION

WWE Universe members were backing The Rock in the finals of the tournament to crown a new WWE Champion at *Survivor Series 1998*. They were left reeling when he turned his back on them and aligned himself with the McMahons, going from The People's Champion to Corporate Champion in one evening.

3 X-PAC BETRAYS KANE

While Kane is typically a loner, he did seem to form a legitimate friendship with his tag team partner X-Pac. The duo captured the World Tag Team Championship twice, but X-Pac cruelly turned on Kane and rejoined his former faction, D-Generation X resulting in a lengthy rivalry between the pair.

4 STONE COLD STEVE AUSTIN'S ALLIANCE

The WWE was fighting for its survival against The Alliance in 2001. It suffered a devastating blow when one of its stars, Stone Cold Steve Austin, chose to take his talents to The Alliance out of pure jealousy of WWE Superstar Kurt Angle.

5 HART FAMILY FEUD

Owen Hart was unhappy that he was not as successful as his older brother Bret. Simmering discontent erupted into outright confrontation when Owen attacked an already injured Bret at the 1994 *Royal Rumble*. The brothers would go on to clash with each other for over a year.

6 STING & THE FOUR HORSEMEN

A brief alliance between Sting and longtime rival Ric Flair brought The Stinger into the Four Horsemen. It didn't last long. When Sting earned a title opportunity against Flair for the NWA World Heavyweight Championship, Flair and the others bounced him right out of the Horsemen.

7

7 EDDIE GUERRERO & REY MYSTERIO

Friends Eddie Guerrero and Rey Mysterio joined forces to win the WWE Tag Team Championship in 2005. When the two later lost the Titles, Guerrero blamed Mysterio. He attacked his friend, igniting a rivalry.

OWEN HART

"I'M FINALLY GONNA GET MY CHANCE."

5

8 STEPHANIE MCMAHON

Mr. McMahon tried to defend the honor of his only daughter, Stephanie, when he thought she'd been duped into marrying the villainous Triple H. But Stephanie didn't need defending. She was clearly happy to be with her new husband—and even happier to turn her back on her father.

9 THE CONCRETE CRYPT

When Undertaker took on The Dudley Boyz in a Concrete Crypt Match at the 2004 *Great American Bash*, his manager and friend, Paul Bearer, faced a grim fate. If The Dudley Boyz won, a glass vault in which he was locked would be filled with concrete. Undertaker won—then filled the vault himself!

10 STING & THE ROAD WARRIORS

Stepping in for Dusty Rhodes, Sting joined The Road Warriors to defend their Six-Man Tag Team Championship against The Varsity Club. But after deciding they were "carrying" Sting, The Road Warriors roughed him up.

1

FIGURE-FOUR LEGLOCK

The Figure-Four gets its name from the shape made by the victim's legs—one bent, one straight. Many Superstars have made this vicious leglock their signature move, including 16-time World Champion Ric Flair. Flair's daughter, Charlotte, modified the move, creating an even more damaging Figure 8.

3

2

SHARPSHOOTER

The Sharpshooter was used by Bret Hart and his niece Natalya to end many matches. They would twist an opponent's legs into a pretzel shape around their own legs, flip the foe over, and put enough pressure on their back to force them to tap out.

7

3

STF

In the Stepover Toehold Facelock (STF) a Superstar traps the ankle of a face-down opponent, then lies on them and pulls their head back hard. The STF has always been acknowledged as a particularly painful move. When practiced with the power of John Cena, it is nothing short of devastating.

4

IRON CLAW

After mastering the powerful Iron Claw, Fritz Von Erich passed the secret of the simple but effective move down to his sons, including NWA Champion Kerry. In it, the aggressor grasps their opponent's head and squeezes with such force that they cannot break free, leaving them begging for mercy.

5

TORTURE RACK

Lex Luger perfected this signature move with his incredible strength. Luger would lift his opponents up, place them across his shoulders, and proceed to bounce them up and down while stretching their entire bodies. There was only one way out—to give in.

6 CAMEL CLUTCH

To inflict the maximum punishment on his foe, The Iron Sheik would straddle their prone body, pull their arms back over his legs, and lock in the Camel Clutch. When the Superstar rocked back, pulling up on his opponent's chin, the pressure on their spines would be increased to an unbearable level.

7 WALLS OF JERICHO

Locking opponents in the Walls of Jericho was hands down Chris Jericho's most popular submission move. As his foe lay face down, he would sit on their spine facing their feet—then bend their legs back mercilessly. The move won him many championships.

8 ANKLE LOCK

Former Olympic wrestler Kurt Angle's favorite submission move was not only ankle-wrenching, but gut-wrenching, too, in its simple brutality. Angle would grab an opponent's foot and twist his ankle with increasing force. Any adversary who did not tap out was in danger of having their ankle snapped.

9 KIMURA LOCK

After softening up his rivals with a variety of painful suplexes, "The Beast" Brock Lesnar put competitors out of their misery with his brutal Kimura Lock. Lesnar's opponent would have to submit quickly to have a chance of avoiding a brutal arm injury.

10 MILLION DOLLAR DREAM

The Sleeper Hold is so-called because it can knock out opponents. Ted DiBiase had his own, devastating version, the Million Dollar Dream, which he used to put down foes completely before arrogantly stuffing banknotes into their mouths.

WHILE MANY MATCHES end in a three-count pinfall, any Superstar will agree that it's much more satisfying to force an opponent to tap out by placing them in a painful hold. Many have a signature submission maneuver that they pull out whenever they want to get their opponents to give up.

TOP 10

MONEY IN THE BANK CASH-INS

INTRODUCED IN 2005 at *WrestleMania 21*, *Money in the Bank* takes the form of a Ladder Match. Suspended above the ring in a briefcase is a contract for a guaranteed championship match that the winner can cash in any time within the year. Many winners have shocked the WWE Universe with their chosen opportunity.

1 — 3.29.2015

SETH ROLLINS
WRESTLEMANIA 31

Seth Rollins was the first to cash in his *Money in the Bank* contract at *WrestleMania*—and the first to do it mid-match. He interjected himself into *WrestleMania 31*'s main event, beating Roman Reigns to win the WWE World Heavyweight Championship.

2 — 1.8.2006

EDGE
NEW YEAR'S REVOLUTION

The first *Money in the Bank* winner, Edge, held onto his title opportunity for 10 months, but the wait was worth it. Edge watched John Cena win an Elimination Chamber Match. He then stepped in and pinned Cena, winning his first WWE Championship.

3 — 6.11.2006

ROB VAN DAM
ECW ONE NIGHT STAND

Rob Van Dam was the first to announce ahead of time where he would cash in. True to his word, Van Dam beat current champ, John Cena, at *One Night Stand*, for the WWE Championship.

4 — 7.18.2010

KANE
MONEY IN THE BANK

Kane became the first winner to cash in his contract on the same night he won it. He waited for Rey Mysterio to defend the World Heavyweight Championship against Jack Swagger. After the match, Kane pinned Mysterio and took the title.

5 — 4.8.2013

DOLPH ZIGGLER
RAW

Dolph Ziggler took advantage of the electric atmosphere and passionate audience at the first *RAW* after *WrestleMania 29* to cash in his *Money in the Bank* opportunity. Ziggler defeated Alberto Del Rio to win the World Heavyweight Championship.

6 DANIEL BRYAN
TABLES, LADDERS, AND CHAIRS

Daniel Bryan is the first to cash in the same contract twice. He first challenged Mark Henry, but his win didn't count because Henry wasn't medically cleared to compete. Bryan then cashed in again to take the World Heavyweight Championship from Big Show.

7 DEAN AMBROSE
MONEY IN THE BANK

After Dean Ambrose won the *Money in the Bank* match, he promised to cash it in on the same night. Ambrose lived up to his word and beat Seth Rollins to become the new WWE Champion.

8 RANDY ORTON
SUMMERSLAM

Three years after he was the victim of a *Money in the Bank* cash-in, Randy Orton used his own. When special guest referee Triple H shocked WWE Champion Daniel Bryan with his dreaded Pedigree maneuver, Orton cashed in and won the title.

9 CM PUNK
EXTREME RULES

CM Punk won *Money in the Bank* at back-to-back *WrestleManias*. In 2008, he cashed in to defeat World Heavyweight Champion Edge. A year later, he cashed in and beat Jeff Hardy just after Hardy won the title, cutting his reign to minutes.

10 THE MIZ
RAW

Randy Orton successfully defended the WWE Championship against Wade Barrett, but was attacked after the match by the entire Nexus group. The Miz saw his chance and cashed in, winning his first WWE Championship.

WWE ANNOUNCER

"MR. MONEY IN THE BANK!"

TOP 10 ROYAL

RUMBLE ROYALTY

THE WWE UNIVERSE eagerly anticipates the first step on the road to *WrestleMania*: the *Royal Rumble*. Winning this contest guarantees the winner a world title opportunity and a spot in *WrestleMania*. But it's a grueling challenge, in which Superstars have to outlast 29 other competitors.

1 STONE COLD STEVE AUSTIN

Stone Cold Steve Austin was the first Superstar to win three Royal Rumble Matches, in 1997, 1998, and 2001. Austin followed up his latter two victories by claiming the WWE Championship, too. His dominance in the Royal Rumble is unrivaled.

2 KANE

Even though he's never won a Royal Rumble Match, Kane has made *Rumble* history. He set the single-match record by eliminating 11 Superstars in 2001—an achievement that held up for 13 years. Kane still holds the career record of more than 40 Royal Rumble eliminations.

3 RIC FLAIR

In 1992, a vacated title meant that the winner of the Royal Rumble Match would also become the new WWE Champion. Ric Flair faced a tough field that included nine former and future world champions, but he managed to win the *Rumble*—and his first WWE Championship.

4 SHAWN MICHAELS

Michaels outlasted 29 competitors to win his first Royal Rumble Match in 1995. He was not able to win the resulting WWE Championship Match, but when he repeated as the *Rumble* winner in 1996, he realized his boyhood dream of becoming the WWE Champion at *WrestleMania XII*.

5 HULK HOGAN

Hulk Hogan won the 1990 event a year after he set a record by eliminating nine Superstars in a Royal Rumble Match that he ultimately lost. Hogan was then able to win a second *Royal Rumble* in 1991, making him the first Superstar to win consecutive Royal Rumble Matches.

6 REY MYSTERIO

Big men tend to be favored in the Royal Rumble Match. So it was a surprise when "The Biggest Little Man" Rey Mysterio lasted more than an hour in the ring and won the 2006 match. Dedicating his effort to his friend Eddie Guerrero, Rey earned the chance to compete at *WrestleMania 22*.

7 TRIPLE H

Triple H punctuated his dramatic return from injury in 2002 by claiming his first *Royal Rumble* victory. Fourteen years later, he became the second Superstar to actually win the WWE World Championship in a Royal Rumble Match, his 14th World Championship.

WWE COMMENTATOR

"NOW TRIPLE H IS GOING TO WRESTLEMANIA."

8 ROMAN REIGNS

Roman Reigns announced his arrival as a future main-eventer in the 2014 *Royal Rumble* by eliminating a record 12 competitors, including his fellow Shield members. Reigns finished as the runner-up that year, but then went on to win the 2015 *Rumble*.

9 CHYNA

Just a few women have competed in the Royal Rumble Match throughout its existence. Not only was Chyna the first to do so, but she also appeared in two consecutive Royal Rumble Matches in 1999 and 2000. She proved herself by eliminating Mark Henry and Chris Jericho, respectively, in each match.

10 JIM DUGGAN

In the first ever Royal Rumble Match in 1988, "Hacksaw" Jim Duggan secured a permanent place in history. Duggan was crowned the first *Royal Rumble* victor when he eliminated the last man left in the ring—the monstrous Superstar, One Man Gang.

TOP 10 SURVIVOR SERIES MOMENTS

SURVIVOR SERIES HAS seen its share of shocking, controversial, and exciting moments. The event, which takes place every November, has introduced some of the most popular Superstars and always delights the WWE Universe.

1 MONTREAL SCREWJOB

Bret Hart defended his WWE Championship in his last match against his longtime rival Shawn Michaels at *Survivor Series 1997*. Under orders from WWE Chairman Mr. McMahon, the referee ended the match by indicating that Hart had submitted when Michaels had him in a hold, even though Hart had not.

2 DEBUT OF UNDERTAKER

At *Survivor Series 1990*, Ted DiBiase revealed a mysterious teammate: a 6-foot 10-inch monster known as Undertaker. Within a minute, Undertaker eliminated Koko B. Ware and soon after eliminated Dusty Rhodes. Undertaker has been a constant dark presence in WWE ever since.

3 WINNER TAKES ALL MATCH

At *Survivor Series 2001*, WWE was embroiled in a civil war as The Alliance, a team of former WCW and ECW Superstars, tried to take over WWE. The main event was a 5-on-5 Elimination Match in which the winner would seize control of WWE. After a bitter struggle, Team WWE won.

4 ANDRE SURVIVES

The Main Event of the first ever *Survivor Series* in 1987 saw two five-man teams captained by Hulk Hogan and Andre the Giant. Andre was the only remaining survivor. He avenged himself against Hogan, who he claimed cheated him out of victory eight months earlier at *WrestleMania III*.

5 ELIMINATION CHAMBER

The Elimination Chamber was introduced for the *RAW* main event of *Survivor Series 2002*. The large steel structure completely enclosed the ring. During its first use, six competitors battled for the World Heavyweight Championship and Shawn Michaels claimed victory.

6 DEBUT OF THE SHIELD

Dean Ambrose, Roman Reigns, and Seth Rollins joined forces to become a new team known as The Shield. They first appeared at *Survivor Series 2012*, and helped CM Punk against Ryback and John Cena. They knocked out Ryback, leaving Punk free to pin down Cena and win the match.

④

7 PUNK'S LENGTHY REIGN

At *Survivor Series 2011*, Alberto Del Rio had to defend the WWE Championship against CM Punk. The two engaged in a lengthy battle, but Punk ultimately won. Punk went on to hold the Title for 14 months—the longest reign in more than a decade.

8 CENA AND THE ROCK

It stunned the WWE Universe to see two bitter rivals, The Rock and John Cena, team up at *Survivor Series 2011*. It was difficult for the pair to set their differences aside, but they worked together to defeat the opposing team of R-Truth and The Miz.

9 KURT ANGLE DEBUTS

Survivor Series 1999 featured the in-ring debut of Kurt Angle, who was the first Olympic gold medalist to compete in WWE. During his first match, Angle, who had won a gold medal in freestyle wrestling at the 1996 Summer Olympic Games, performed an Angle Slam against his opponent to win.

10 WHO'S NEXT?

After 12 years removed from competition, Goldberg returned to WWE to answer a challenge from Brock Lesnar at *Survivor Series 2016*. Expecting a back-and-forth slugfest, the WWE Universe was stunned when Goldberg pinned Lesnar 84 seconds into the match.

⑩

1 THE ROAD WARRIORS' SHOULDER PADS

The large spikes protruding from the Road Warriors' shoulder pads added to their ominous appearance.

2 RAZOR RAMON'S TOOTHPICK

Ramon strutted toward the ring chewing on a toothpick like a typical movie star rebel. Once in the ring, he would often throw it at his opponent before the match.

3 CHARLOTTE'S ROBES

Following in the footsteps of her father, "Nature Boy" Ric Flair, Charlotte adds a touch of class to her ring approach by wearing long sparkly robes.

4 BOOGEYMAN'S ALARM CLOCK

The disturbed Superstar carried an oversized alarm clock during his creepy approach to the ring. He'd then smash the clock on his own head before the match.

5 JERRY LAWLER'S CROWN

Many Superstars have claimed to be royalty, but none have carried a crown to the ring for as long as Jerry "The King" Lawler who has reigned over sports entertainment since the 1970s.

6 TRIPLE H'S WATER BOTTLE

Triple H's clear water bottle is a simple accessory, but it is used for dramatic effect before matches. He takes a gulp from it before leaning back and spraying water into the air.

7 ASUKA'S MASK AND ROBE

Asuka wears a white mask and multicolored full-length robe to the ring. Her flamboyant entrance riles up the crowd and her fans also wear the iconic mask to show their support.

TOP 10 ENTRANCE ACCESSORIES

FOR MANY SUPERSTARS throughout sports entertainment history, it is not enough to simply walk to the ring. A Superstar's arrival for battle must have style and pizazz to rattle and impress their opponents.

HACKSAW JIM DUGGAN'S TRUSTY 2X4 8 ▶

Duggan carried a 2x4 piece of wood to help him get through the legions of supporters who fervently cheered him on before every match.

JBL'S 10-GALLON HAT 10 ▲

Everything about JBL's arrival to the ring was about portraying power and wealth—from his luxurious limo to his extra-large 10-gallon hat.

◀ 9 **HULK HOGAN'S FEATHER BOA**

Hulk Hogan's bold arrival outfit included a bandanna and a striking feather boa.

TOP 10 UNUSUAL MATCHES

MOST MATCHES IN SPORTS entertainment are contested under normal rules. In order to win, Superstars must either pin their opponent or force them to submit, while avoiding a count out or disqualification. Occasionally though, unusual matches are set with strange rules to excite the **WWE Universe**.

RICK MARTEL IN A BLINDFOLD MATCH AT *WRESTLEMANIA XII* 03.24.1991

Jerry Lawler lost to Bret Hart in a Kiss My Foot Match at *King of the Ring 1995.*

1 SCAFFOLD MATCH

High above the ring, Superstars competed on a narrow plank with the goal being to knock the other Superstar off.

2 EMPTY ARENA MATCH

To prevent audience interference, some important matches have been contested in an empty arena.

3 SPIN THE WHEEL, MAKE THE DEAL

In 1992 and 1993, *Halloween Havoc* featured a roulette wheel that determined which of 12 different match types would be fought.

4 KISS MY FOOT MATCH

The loser was forced to kiss the winner's foot.

5 WORLD WAR 3

A World War 3 match needed three rings to accommodate the sixty Superstars who took part.

6 BURIED ALIVE MATCH

To win this match a Superstar had to bury their opponent under a mound of dirt.

7 DOG COLLAR MATCH

Both competitors wore dog collars that were connected to each other by a chain.

8 JINGLE BELLES

Wearing festive clothes, two teams of six female Superstars took part in this Christmas clash.

9 BLINDFOLD MATCH

Both competitors have to wear blindfolds during these matches and rely on their other senses.

10 CHAMPIONSHIP SCRAMBLE

Featuring five Superstars, any pinfall or submission resulted in a new champion. Once the allotted match time ran out the final champion walked away as the winner.

TOP 10 MOMENTS IN RAW HISTORY

RAW BEGAN AS A TAPED one-hour program and expanded to two hours on Monday night. The show then became a three-hour live spectacle, which showcased the biggest current Superstars. It has provided incredible matches and unforgettable moments for almost a quarter of a century.

1 MR. MCMAHON BUYS WCW

WWE purchased WCW and decided to end WCW's rival show, *Nitro*. WWE Chairman Mr. McMahon made an announcement in a simultaneous transmission on *RAW* and *Nitro*, but his victorious speech soured when he learned that his son, Shane, was actually the McMahon who owned WCW.

2 "THIS IS YOUR LIFE"

Mankind looked to cement his tag team partnership with The Rock by ingratiating him with a "This Is Your Life" segment on *RAW*. Unfortunately, The Rock held grudges with all of the figures Mankind brought from his past and proceeded to hurl entertaining retorts at each guest.

3 THE ULTIMATE SPEECH

Newly inducted into the Hall of Fame, the Ultimate Warrior made his return to *RAW* and thanked the WWE Universe for all the love and support they had shown him over the years. It was a powerful and emotional speech that took on an additional air of sadness when the Warrior passed away the next day.

4 MCMAHON & BISCHOFF UNITED

When Eric Bischoff ran WCW, he spent years trying to put Mr. McMahon and WWE out of business. But on a July 2002 episode of *RAW*, Mr. McMahon announced that he had made a lucrative business decision: he'd hired Bischoff to be the new general manager of *RAW*.

5 THE ALLIANCE FORMS

Former ECW Superstars were trying to wreak havoc by invading *RAW*. WWE and WCW decided to combine forces to solve the problem with their Superstars, but this was a double-cross. ECW and WCW formed an alliance and came dangerously close to shutting down WWE permanently.

6 PIPE BOMB PROMO

CM Punk was planning to leave WWE in July 2011 and felt he had nothing to lose. So the disgruntled Superstar decided to let everyone know how he really felt about WWE, the McMahons, and his fellow competitors in a scathing tirade later dubbed a verbal "pipe bomb" on *RAW*.

7

7 THE BEER TRUCK

The Corporation stable was celebrating their new partnership with The Rock after they helped him become WWE Champion when they received a surprise visit. Set to challenge for the Championship, Stone Cold Steve Austin drove a beer truck to the ring and hosed down the group.

8 THE CHAMP ARRIVES

The 2005 WWE Draft has proven to be the most significant in *RAW*'s history. With the #1 overall pick, Eric Bischoff made a major splash by picking the current WWE Champion John Cena. While serving as *RAW*'s marque Superstar, Cena went on to win fourteen additional World Titles.

9 A NEW DX

Shawn Michaels lost the WWE Championship at *WrestleMania XIV* and retired from WWE. The next night on *RAW*, Triple H took charge of his stable, D-Generation X, stealing X-Pac from WCW and recruiting the tag team, The New Age Outlaws.

3

10 FLAIR'S FAREWELL

Before Flair's retirement following his loss to Shawn Michaels at *WrestleMania XXIV*, he gave an emotional farewell speech on *RAW*. Flair was surrounded by current and retired Superstars who came to honor one of the greatest careers in sports entertainment.

TOP 10 AUTHORITY FIGURES

SPORTS ENTERTAINMENT takes a lot of organizing. While focusing on growing WWE into a global power, Mr. McMahon and his family have often put proxy figures in charge of the day-to-day operation of *SmackDown* and *RAW*. But keeping Superstars in line is never an easy task.

1 ERIC BISCHOFF

The WWE Universe was stunned when Mr. McMahon hired former rival and WCW boss Eric Bischoff to be the *RAW* General Manager. Bischoff held the position for several years, before being fired in December 2005. Mr. McMahon ended Bischoff's tenure by asking John Cena to "take out the trash."

2 PAUL HEYMAN

Heyman joined WWE in 2001 as an announcer. He later became General Manager of *SmackDown*, and has since held various positions of power in WWE. Famed for his no-nonsense attitude and brash, fast-talking delivery, this powerful man is someone no Superstar wants to get on the wrong side of.

3 VICKIE GUERRERO

General Manager Vickie Guerrero ran *SmackDown* and *RAW* at different times from 2007 to 2014. Her tendency to favor Superstars she was romantically involved with did not go down well, nor did her habit of booking her nephew, Chavo Guerrero, Jr., in favorable matches.

4 TEDDY LONG

Long served as an official and a manager before becoming the longest-serving *SmackDown* General Manager from 2004 to 2008. Unlike many others, Long was a fair leader who tried to even out advantages he felt were earned by cheating. He held a variety of authoritative positions until 2013.

5 WILLIAM REGAL

Regal became Commissioner of *RAW* in 2001, a position he held for nearly a year. In 2014, Regal became the General Manager of NXT, where he has been molding the next generation of WWE Superstars, including many from the international circuit.

6 JACK TUNNEY

In 1984, Jack Tunney became President of WWE (the equivalent of today's General Manager) and held that role for more than a decade. Unlike many of the authority figures that followed him, Tunney favored neither good guys nor bad guys, but seemed to remain neutral in all his decisions.

1

7 MICK FOLEY

Foley became Commissioner of WWE in 2000, after retiring from in-ring competition. He was fired by Mr. McMahon at the end of the year, but briefly served in the role again in 2001. Most recently, the popular Foley was named the General Manager of *RAW*.

8 GORILLA MONSOON

When Jack Tunney's decade-long tenure as WWE President ended in 1995, WWE Hall of Famer Monsoon took over. This tough but fair leader was the last WWE President. After he retired in 1997, WWE changed the title of the person scheduling matches and disciplining Superstars to Commissioner.

JOHN LAURINAITIS

"DON'T MAKE ME TAKE OFF MY JACKET."

9 SHAWN MICHAELS

Michaels served as WWE Commissioner for two years during his four-year retirement from the ring. First siding with Mr. McMahon's Corporation Superstars, he later became a thorn in the WWE Chairman's side by making Mr. McMahon enter the 1999 *Royal Rumble* match in an unfavorable position.

10

10 JOHN LAURINAITIS

Laurinaitis was a General Manager of first *RAW* and then *SmackDown*. He surrounded himself with powerful advisers and called himself "Big Johnny," but no amount of bigging up could help him hold on to his position. Mr. McMahon fired Laurinaitis in 2012.

TOP 10

WRESTLEMANIA PERFORMERS

IF THERE'S ONE EVENT THE WWE Universe looks forward to, it's *WrestleMania*. With the biggest and best moves and incredible matches, every Superstar wants to shine in the ring during the "Show of Shows." Some Superstars have gone above and beyond to leave a lasting impression long after the bright lights of *WrestleMania* have faded.

1 SHAWN MICHAELS

Shawn Michaels (aka "Mr. *WrestleMania*") has competed in 17 *WrestleManias*, and several of his matches rank among the greatest in *WrestleMania* history. His Ladder Match for the Intercontinental Championship against Razor Ramon at *WrestleMania X* was one of the first of its kind. Michaels won his first WWE Championship at *WrestleMania XII*, defeating Bret "Hit Man" Hart in a 60-minute Iron Man Match.

2 UNDERTAKER

Undertaker dominated WWE Hall of Famer "Superfly" Jimmy Snuka at *WrestleMania VII*. The Dead Man continued to impress fans, winning an incomparable 21 *WrestleManias* in a row. Though "The Streak" is over, Undertaker walked away from *WrestleMania 32* with an amazing lifetime record of 23 wins and just one loss.

WWE ANNOUNCER, MICHAEL COLE

"SHATTERED DREAMS LAY IN HIS WAKE."

3 HULK HOGAN

Hulk Hogan competed in the main event of seven of the first eight *WrestleManias*. His partnership with Hollywood star Mr. T brought significant mainstream publicity to the first *WrestleMania*, and helped the annual tradition get off to an incredible start.

4 STONE COLD STEVE AUSTIN

Austin gave the WWE Universe some of the most memorable moments in *WrestleMania* history. From his stunning resilience against Bret Hart at *WrestleMania 13*, to epic battles with his rival, The Rock, Steve Austin knew how to "stomp a mud hole" on the Grandest Stage, winning the WWE Championship three times at *WrestleMania* events.

5 TRIPLE H

No one has competed in more World Championship Matches at *WrestleMania* than Triple H. In his career he defeated three other Superstars in a Fatal 4-Way Elimination Match at *WrestleMania 2000* and pinned Chris Jericho to become the second Undisputed Champion ever at *WrestleMania X8*.

CONTINUED

6 JOHN CENA

Cena first appeared in the opening match of *WrestleMania XX*, where he defeated Big Show for the United States Championship. The following year, Cena captured the WWE Championship for the first time in his storied career. Over the years, Cena has fought for world championships against an incredible collection of legendary Superstars, including Triple H, Shawn Michaels, Batista, Edge, Randy Orton, and The Rock.

7 EDGE

After Edge and his tag team partner, Christian, beat their rivals the Hardys and Dudleys in a Ladder Match and *Tables, Ladders, and Chairs* match at consecutive *WrestleMania* events, Edge went on to make history again by winning the inaugural *Money in the Bank* match at *WrestleMania 21*. The last match of his career was a successful title defense at *WrestleMania XXVII*.

8 RANDY SAVAGE

Only one competitor has won four matches at a single *WrestleMania* event, and that was the Macho Man Randy Savage. Competing in the one-day tournament for the vacant WWE Championship at *WrestleMania IV*, Savage had to defeat Butch Reed, Greg Valentine, One Man Gang, and Ted DiBiase to win his first WWE Championship. One year earlier, Savage faced Ricky "The Dragon" Steamboat in a match many consider the greatest in *WrestleMania* history.

9 BRET "HIT MAN" HART

Bret "Hit Man" Hart competed in 12 consecutive *WrestleMania* events. In this time, he became the first man to compete in matches for the Intercontinental Championship (*WrestleMania VIII*), the Tag Team Championship (*WrestleMania VII*), and the **WWE** Championship (*WrestleMania IX, X, and XII*).

10 THE ROCK

The Rock has competed in nine *WrestleMania* events—four of them being for the WWE Championship. He has won several titles and he is the only Superstar in the history of WWE to face—and beat—Hulk Hogan, Stone Cold Steve Austin, and John Cena at the Showcase of the Immortals.

1

5

1 KANE'S DEBUT

10.5.1997

The first Hell in a Cell match was partially designed to let Shawn Michaels and Undertaker compete without interference from the stable, D-Generation X. But Kane, Undertaker's brother, broke in and attacked his brother—helping Michaels win.

2 MANKIND'S CELL DROP

6.28.1998

Mankind and Undertaker decided to begin their match on top of the cell instead of inside it. Undertaker managed to toss Mankind off the top of the cell, sending him crashing through the announcers' table more than 16-feet below.

3 HOT CHOKESLAM

8.17.2008

SummerSlam 2008 was over—but Undertaker decided to dole out more punishment to the man he defeated, Edge. Undertaker threw Edge off a ladder with a chokeslam at such force, he went through the mat below. Then the ring burst into flames!

4 MR. MCMAHON'S REAR VIEW

9.17.2006

WWE boss Mr. McMahon, his son, Shane McMahon, and Big Show tried to beat D-Generation X in a 3-on-2 Handicap Hell in a Cell match. But D-Generation X embarrassed the Chairman of WWE by pushing his face into Big Show's rear end before winning the match.

5 SHANE'S LEAP OF FAITH

4.3.2016

The stakes were high at *WrestleMania 32*: Mr. McMahon claimed Shane McMahon could control *RAW* if he won a Hell in a Cell match against Undertaker. So Shane took a big risk, leaping onto Undertaker from the top of the cell. He missed and lost the match.

6 CHAIR ATTACK

6.26.2005

Triple H wanted his World Heavyweight Championship back from Batista and was willing to do anything to make it happen, including attacking the Champion with a chair wrapped in barbed wire. But even this couldn't help Triple H reclaim the Title.

7 THE CROOKED OFFICIAL

10.28.2012

Ryback earned a WWE Championship shot thanks to his extended undefeated streak. It looked like he would win the match, but a crooked official, Brad Maddox, who wanted to become a Superstar, refused to count a pin and helped CM Punk retain the Title.

8 THE SUPERPLEX ONTO CHAIRS

10.27.2013

With the WWE Championship on the line, Randy Orton tried to finish Daniel Bryan off by delivering a devastating superplex move: flipping Daniel Bryan backward off the top rope onto a pile of chairs the Superstars had brought into the ring.

9 EDGE SPEARS UNDERTAKER

8.17.2008

Edge demonstrated he could take on the fearsome Undertaker by flooring his opponent with his signature spear move. Edge charged at Undertaker, slamming his shoulder into him and sending them both crashing through the cell wall.

10 SIX MEN IN ONE CELL

12.10.2000

Chaos reigned when Kurt Angle faced five other men in a 6-Man Hell in a Cell Match for the WWE Championship. The official had no chance of control over the zealous competitors, who clashed inside and outside the ring for the entire bout.

HELL IN A CELL MATCHES are some of the most brutal. In these heated battles, Superstars compete while locked inside a huge metal structure. The fierce bouts that ensue have been known to alter careers, as the prospects of those who dare to step inside the cell are changed once and for all.

TOP 10

SUPERSTAR CATCHPHRASES

Some of the greatest Superstars are best remembered for their quotes and catchphrases.

1 **"TO BE THE MAN, YOU GOTTA BEAT THE MAN."** Ric Flair riled up opponents with his catchphrase, telling them that he would come out on top as "the man" when all was said and done.

2 **"AND THAT'S THE BOTTOM LINE, 'CUZ STONE COLD SAYS SO."** There was no changing Stone Cold Steve Austin's mind when he used this line on competitors. Austin always had the last word.

3 **"WHATCHA GONNA DO WHEN HULKAMANIA RUNS WILD ON YOU, BROTHER?"** Hulk Hogan warned opponents that his fans' frenzied enthusiasm was as powerful as he was himself.

4 **"IF YOU SMELL WHAT THE ROCK IS COOKING."** The WWE Universe echoes The Rock's signature phrase, showing their support for the Superstar.

5 **"THE BEST THERE IS, THE BEST THERE WAS, THE BEST THERE EVER WILL BE."** Bret "Hit Man" Hart wasn't humble when he talked himself up to future opponents.

6 **"YOU CAN'T SEE ME!"** John Cena's catchphrase tells opponents that they are not on his level.

7 **"YES! YES! YES!"** Originally meant to taunt crowds, Daniel Bryan's "Yes! Yes! Yes!" chant evolved into a rallying cry for Bryan and the WWE Universe.

8 **"WHO'S NEXT?"** Goldberg dared Superstar after Superstar to challenge him with this signature phrase.

9 **"WHAT A RUSH!"** The gutteral sound of the Road Warrior's famous line signaled that the tag team was on their way to the ring.

10 **"REST IN PEACE!"** A master of horror, Undertaker promised doom for his opponents when he delivered this ominous warning.

TOP 10
MEMORABLE INSULTS

Superstars have verbally dominated in the ring with some impressive put-downs.

1 **"I WILL NEVER FORGIVE YOUR MOTHER FOR GIVING BIRTH TO YOU!"** Mr. McMahon to his son, Shane

2 **"I'M BROCK LESNAR / HERE COMES THE PAIN / GOD MADE ME STRONG / FORGOT TO GIVE ME BRAIN!"** John Cena raps to Brock Lesnar

3 **"YOU SOUND LIKE A HUMAN VACUUM CLEANER; MANAGING TO SUCK AND BLOW AT THE SAME TIME!"** Edge to Billy Gunn

4 **"WITHOUT UGLY IN THE WORLD, THERE'D BE NO BEAUTY. SO, LUKE GALLOWS, THANKS FOR YOUR SACRIFICE."** Enzo Amore to Luke Gallows

5 **"ISN'T IT WEIRD HOW YOUR BROTHER AND YOUR FATHER LOOK NOTHING ALIKE?"** Chris Jericho to Dean Malenko

6 **"THE ONLY REASON YOU WERE CHAMPION FOR A YEAR IS BECAUSE TRIPLE H DIDN'T WANT TO WORK TUESDAYS!"** Paul Heyman to JBL

7 **"THIS SHIRT IS A PARODY OF YOU BECAUSE I THINK YOU ARE A PARODY OF WRESTLING!"** Daniel Bryan to John Cena

8 **"I BET YOUR FATHER IS CALLING HIS LAWYER RIGHT NOW TRYING TO FIND A LOOPHOLE IN YOUR BIRTH CERTIFICATE."** Jerry Lawler to Al Jackson

9 **"IF YOU WERE ON LIFE SUPPORT, I'D PULL THE PLUG AND CHARGE MY IPHONE."** JBL to Bryon Saxton

10 **"I'M GONNA TAKE CARE OF THAT SMELLY, NASTY, GREASY ANIMAL… AND I'M GONNA GET YOU, TOO, RHYNO!"** Chris Jericho to Stephanie McMahon and Rhyno

John Cena and Daniel Bryan

Hulk Hogan (left); The Rock (above)

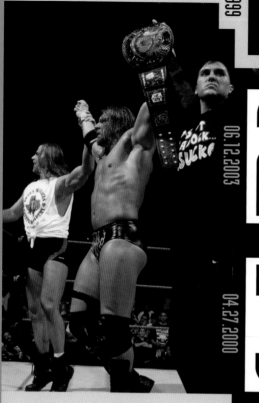

1 — TRIPLE H VS. THE ROCK
08.26.1999

The first regularly scheduled episode of *SmackDown* featured WWE Champion Triple H against The Rock, with Shawn Michaels as a special guest referee. It seemed like The Rock was going to win, until Michaels superkicked him and knocked him out, helping his ally Triple H, retain the Title.

2 — COLLAPSED RING
06.12.2003

A match between Big Show and Brock Lesnar featured a famously destructive moment. With Show on the top turnbuckle, Lesnar delivered a superplex, throwing the 500-pound Show over his shoulders, but as they crashed down, the ring collapsed—the power and weight of the duo was just too much.

3 — DX EXPRESS NO MORE
04.27.2000

Originally an anti-authority faction, D-Generation X changed course and aligned themselves with WWE owners, the McMahons. As a perk, the group were given a luxurious bus to travel in until Stone Cold Steve Austin destroyed the bus on *SmackDown* by dropping a metal girder on it, causing it to explode!

4 — A ROOKIE'S RISE
06.27.2002

Kurt Angle issued an open challenge to battle with any competitor on *SmackDown*. Rookie John Cena responded to the challenge. Angle pinned the inexperienced Superstar, but Cena's show of bravery jump-started his ascent to the top of WWE.

5 — IRON MEN
09.18.2003

Brock Lesnar and Kurt Angle fought for the WWE Championship on *SmackDown*. The 60-minute Iron Man match, which only ends at the allotted time, rather than with a pin or submission, was fierce and intense. Lesnar battled through to win the match 5-4 and became WWE Champion once again.

6 BROCK LESNAR VS. HULK HOGAN

08.08.2002

2002 King of the Ring Brock Lesnar faced off against Hulk Hogan and clinched the victory by forcing the legend to submit. This earned him an Undisputed Championship Match against The Rock.

7 THE SHIELD VS. UNDERTAKER

04.26.2013

A notable *SmackDown* episode featured Dean Ambrose facing Undertaker. Although Undertaker won the match, Ambrose's stable mates from The Shield, Seth Rollins and Roman Reigns, attacked Undertaker and put him through a table.

8 SUPERMARKET SCRAMBLE

12.13.2001

There have been wild brawls between Superstars both in the ring and backstage, but in December 2001, Stone Cold Steve Austin and Booker T took their rivalry to a local supermarket. They fought their way through the aisles, causing havoc as they went. Austin was the overall winner.

9 A NEW DRAFT

07.19.2016

In 2016, *SmackDown* became a weekly live show and the first episode featured the 2016 WWE Draft. *RAW*'s authority figures, Stephanie McMahon and Mick Foley, picked Seth Rollins first. Their counterparts, Shane McMahon and Daniel Bryan, chose WWE Champion Dean Ambrose.

10 DEADLY HUMOR

03.27.2009

On a *SmackDown* episode leading up to *WrestleMania 25*, Shawn Michaels entered in the style of Undertaker amidst smoke and hooded figures. The subject of his mockery then rose demonically out of the smoke and grabbed him!

INTRODUCED IN 1999, *SmackDown* soon joined *RAW* as weekly viewing for the WWE Universe. The show has featured its own championships and Superstars. Some of the most bizarre and controversial moments in the past two decades of WWE have occurred on *SmackDown*.

3

5

1

3.23.1997

BRET HART VS. STONE COLD STEVE AUSTIN

After months of animosity, Stone Cold Steve Austin and Bret Hart met in a Submissions Match at *WrestleMania 13*. The bout ended without either man giving in—Austin passed out, forcing the official, UFC star Ken Shamrock, to call the match.

2

3.30.2008

SHAWN MICHAELS VS. RIC FLAIR

Shawn Michaels faced the legendary Ric Flair at *WrestleMania XXIV* in a match that put Flair's career on the line. Michaels mouthed, "I love you" to Flair before delivering the devastating Sweet Chin Music move that lead to Flair's final defeat.

3

6.28.1998

UNDERTAKER VS. MANKIND

Some of the most iconic moments in Mankind's career occurred during the 1998 Hell in a Cell Match. Undertaker threw him off the cage, through it, and onto a blanket of thumbtacks. Mankind received a standing ovation from the crowd upon losing.

4

3.17.2002

"HOLLYWOOD" HULK HOGAN VS. THE ROCK

Even though the villainous "Hollywood" Hulk Hogan was battling "The People's Champ" The Rock at *WrestleMania X8*, there was excitement for Hogan's first *WrestleMania* appearance in almost a decade. The Rock won, but the crowd cheered both men.

5

3.24.1991

ULTIMATE WARRIOR VS. RANDY SAVAGE

After Randy Savage caused The Ultimate Warrior to lose the WWE Championship, they decided WWE wasn't big enough for them both. They met in a Retirement Match at *WrestleMania VII*—forcing Savage to quit.

6 THE HART FOUNDATION VS. TEAM AUSTIN

7.06.1997

Bret Hart's new Canadian faction, The Hart Foundation, defeated Stone Cold Steve Austin's squad, Team Austin, in an action-packed 10-Man Tag Team Match in front of a charged Calgary crowd at *In Your House 16: Canadian Stampede*.

7 MR. PERFECT VS. RIC FLAIR

1.25.1993

In the early days of *Monday Night RAW*, two former-friends-turned-bitter-rivals met in a high-stakes match: the loser had to leave WWE. Mr. Perfect was victorious, and Flair returned to his long time home, WCW.

8 TRIPLE H VS. SHAWN MICHAELS

8.25.2002

During a seemingly joyous reunion after Michaels returned from retirement in 2002, Triple H brutally attacked him, spurring an Unsanctioned Match at *SummerSlam*. Michaels won, and a bitter Triple H attacked him again, this time with a sledgehammer.

9 SHANE MCMAHON VS. KURT ANGLE

6.24.2001

Shane McMahon rudely interrupted Kurt Angle during a ceremony and ignited a dispute between the two Superstars. McMahon and Angle met in a No-Holds-Barred Street Fight where Angle threw Shane through two glass walls en route to victory.

10 SGT. SLAUGHTER VS. PAT PATTERSON

5.04.1981

The fiendish Sgt. Slaughter began a rivalry with Superstar-turned-commentator Pat Patterson when he called him a coward. Patterson settled things in an Alley Fight at WWE's unofficial home, Madison Square Garden.

WHILE CHAMPIONSHIP MATCHES are exciting with obvious stakes on the line, Superstars often fight for other reasons—whether it's to strengthen a case for a future championship opportunity, test themselves against fellow competitors, or to settle a longstanding grudge.

TOP 10
LADDER MATCHES

During a Ladder Match a valuable possession, such as a championship, is suspended high above the ring. Superstars must battle to be the first to grab the prize.

1 CHRIS JERICHO VS. SHAWN MICHAELS, *NO MERCY* [October 5, 2008] Chris Jericho successfully defended the World Heavyweight Championship against rival Shawn Michaels.

2 TRIPLE H VS. THE ROCK, *SUMMERSLAM* [August 30, 1998] The Rock lost the Intercontinental Championship against a victorious Triple H.

3 MONEY IN THE BANK, *WRESTLEMANIA 21* [April 3, 2005] Edge outlasted Chris Jericho, Shelton Benjamin, Kane, Chris Benoit, and Christian to win the first *Money in the Bank* Ladder Match.

4 SHAWN MICHAELS VS. RAZOR RAMON, *WRESTLEMANIA X* [March 20, 1994] Michaels also kept the Intercontinental Championship in an encore match against Razor Ramon at *SummerSlam 1995*.

5 FINN BALOR VS. KEVIN OWENS, *NXT TAKEOVER: BROOKLYN* [August 22, 2015] Owens failed to regain the NXT Championship.

6 CHRIS JERICHO VS. CHRIS BENOIT, *ROYAL RUMBLE* [January 21, 2001] The Intercontinental Championship went to Chris Jericho at the 2001 *Royal Rumble*.

7 ROB VAN DAM VS. JEFF HARDY, *RAW* [July 22, 2002] Van Dam scaled the ladder to unify the European and Intercontinental Championships.

8 MR. MCMAHON & SHANE MCMAHON VS. STONE COLD STEVE AUSTIN, *KING OF THE RING* [June 27, 1999] With control of WWE at stake, father and son teamed up against Austin and won.

9 THE ROCK VS. MANKIND, *RAW* [February 15, 1999] The Rock gained the WWE Championship from bitter rival, Mankind.

10 UNDERTAKER VS. JEFF HARDY, *RAW* [July 1, 2002] Hardy tested Undertaker, but couldn't win the Undisputed Championship.

Chris Jericho and Shawn Michaels try to grab the World Heavyweight Championship title.

TOP 10 TOUGHEST MATCHES

Some match stipulations push Superstars past their usual limits.

1 TRIPLE H VS. SHAWN MICHAELS [August 25, 2002] Michaels made his return at this ferocious, Unsanctioned Street Fight against his former best friend, Triple H.

2 DUSTY RHODES VS. "SUPERSTAR" BILLY GRAHAM [October 24, 1977] Graham narrowly won this Texas Death Match when Rhodes succumbed to a pinfall.

3 TERRY FUNK VS. RIC FLAIR [November 15, 1989] Flair dealt out so much punishment, Funk said, "I quit!" to end the match.

4 JOHN CENA VS. RANDY ORTON [October 25, 2009] As if a 60-minute Iron Man Match wasn't enough, an "anything goes" stipulation allowed for submissions outside the ropes, too.

5 JBL VS. BIG SHOW [February 20, 2005] With barbed wire atop the Steel Cage for the first time, JBL escaped by tunneling under the ring.

6 ROB VAN DAM VS. SABU [August 3, 1996] Van Dam was incapacitated and carried off in this Stretcher Match.

7 SGT. SLAUGHTER VS. PAT PATTERSON [May 4, 1981] Patterson used his belt and boot to secure this Alley Fight win.

8 KURT ANGLE VS. SHANE MCMAHON [June 24, 2001] Angle won the brutal Street Fight after tossing Shane McMahon through panes of clear plastic—twice.

9 TRIPLE H VS. CACTUS JACK [February 27, 2000] Barbed wire and thumbtacks were used in a Hell in a Cell Match that forced Cactus Jack to lose and retire.

10 EDGE & CHRISTIAN VS. THE HARDYS VS. THE DUDLEYS [August 27, 2000] All six men crashed through tables, soared off ladders, and felt the impact of steel chairs.

1

SHAWN
MICHAELS

"I RESPECT THE
UNDERTAKER BUT
I AM NOT AFRAID."

1 WRESTLEMANIA 25
VS. SHAWN MICHAELS

Shawn Michaels tried to live up to his *"Mr. WrestleMania"* moniker by defeating Undertaker, but lost in an energetic encounter that saw a cameraman and a referee get caught in the crossfire.

2 WRESTLEMANIA 30
VS. BROCK LESNAR

Paul Heyman assured everyone Lesnar would be the one to end Undertaker's 21-match *WrestleMania* winning streak. But when Lesnar actually pinned Undertaker to make his record 21-1, Heyman and the WWE Universe were in shock.

3 WRESTLEMANIA XIV
VS. KANE

Undertaker's estranged manager, Paul Bearer, shocked him by bringing Undertaker's brother, Kane, into WWE. Undertaker initially refused to battle "his own flesh and blood," but was forced into pinning Kane in an intense match.

4 WRESTLEMANIA 23
VS. BATISTA

When Undertaker won the 2007 *Royal Rumble* Match, he earned a *WrestleMania 23* title match against World Heavyweight Champion Batista. Undertaker defeated Batista in a back-and-forth slugfest and won the title for the first time.

5 WRESTLEMANIA XXVIII
VS. TRIPLE H

After Triple H nearly defeated Undertaker at *WrestleMania XXVII*, a rematch was made the following year. Despite inflicting considerable punishment on Undertaker, Triple H fell short. The rivals showed respect by walking off together.

6 WRESTLEMANIA XXVI
VS. SHAWN MICHAELS

After losing to Undertaker at *WrestleMania 25*, Shawn Michaels pledged to defeat him. Undertaker offered Michaels another shot—if he put his career on the line. Michaels agreed but lost the match, ending his storied career.

7 WRESTLEMANIA XXIV
VS. EDGE

Undertaker fought for a World Championship for the third time during his 21-match winning streak at *WrestleMania XXIV*. The Superstar took on Edge to win the World Heavyweight Championship for the second time.

8 WRESTLEMANIA 21
VS. RANDY ORTON

Former WWE Champion, Billy Graham, suggested to Randy Orton that challenging Undertaker would help his reputation. Undertaker accepted the match, and despite inteference from Orton's father, "Cowboy" Bob Orton, he pinned his opponent.

9 WRESTLEMANIA VIII
VS. JAKE "THE SNAKE" ROBERTS

Undertaker's second appearance and win at *WrestleMania* came against Jake "The Snake" Roberts. The former allies became rivals when Undertaker would not allow the disturbed Superstar to attack Randy Savage's wife, Miss Elizabeth.

10 WRESTLEMANIA X8
VS. RIC FLAIR

After Ric Flair became co-owner of WWE in late 2001, Flair and Undertaker clashed, resulting in a match. Despite assistance from Superstar Arn Anderson, Flair couldn't beat the Undertaker, who extended his streak to 10-0.

PERHAPS NO FEAT IN WWE is as impressive as Undertaker's legendary *WrestleMania* streak of 21 straight wins. As the list of his victims grew, more Superstars stepped up to try to bring an end to Undertaker's success. But his record continued to grow for more than two decades.

TOP 10 ELIMINATION CHAMBER MOMENTS

11.17.2002

1 SHAWN MICHAELS WINS THE FIRST ELIMINATION CHAMBER

Shawn Michaels completed his unlikely return to the ring after more than four years by defeating his five opponents and winning the World Heavyweight Championship in the inaugural Elimination Chamber Match at *Survivor Series 2002*.

2.15.2009

2 TWO CHAMBER MATCHES IN ONE NIGHT

After Edge lost his WWE Championship in the first Elimination Chamber match of the night at *No Way Out 2009*, the opportunistic Superstar jumped Kofi Kingston to steal his spot in the second, winning the match and the World Heavyweight Championship.

2.20.2011

3 FROM THE TOP

At *Elimination Chamber 2011*, six Superstars fought for a chance to face The Miz at *WrestleMania XXVII*. The stakes were high, but John Morrison climbed higher. He climbed to the chamber's top and fell on Sheamus—eliminating him. Morrison was eliminated, too, and John Cena went on to win the match.

2.21.2010

4 OUTSIDE INTERFERENCE

While one would imagine that the steel-linked cage would prevent outside interference by other Superstars, this isn't always the case. Shawn Michaels broke into the cage for the 2010 match for the World Heavyweight Championship, causing Undertaker to lose the Title to Chris Jericho.

12.3.2006

5 LASHLEY GETS THE TABLE

The first Extreme Elimination Chamber Match took place in 2006. Fighting for the ECW World Championship, each pod held a Superstar and an object. Bobby Lashley used his table to break the top of his pod, he then climbed out and eliminated two men on his way to taking the Title.

INTRODUCED IN 2002, the Elimination Chamber is a steel cage that encloses the ring. It has six pods and each pod holds a competitor. Two Superstars start the match and the others enter at timed intervals. The competitors must pin or submit their opponents to eliminate them and win.

6 TRIPLE POD

5.31.2015

When defending their Tag Team Championship, New Day had to face five other teams in a team Elimination Chamber Match. They had two advantages—they entered the match last, and all three members of the team were able to compete. With numbers in their favor, they retained the Title.

4

7 THROWN OFF THE POD

2.17.2008

Fighting for a World Heavyweight Title Match at *WrestleMania XXIV*, Montel Vontavious Porter looked to finish off Undertaker with a high-risk move from the top of a pod in the Elimination Chamber. But Undertaker followed him, and threw him down to the ring.

8 PUNK'S POD DOOR STUCK

2.20.2011

At *Elimination Chamber 2011*, CM Punk's pod door would not fully open. He got stuck and Randy Orton attacked him and pulled him out of his pod, eliminating Punk. The *RAW* General Manager decided that was unfair and put Punk back in the match. Punk eliminated Orton but lost the match.

3

9 GAME OVER

8.24.2003

Goldberg dominated the Elimination Chamber Match for the World Heavyweight Championship at *SummerSlam 2003*, eliminating Randy Orton, Shawn Michaels, and Chris Jericho in just over two minutes. But Triple H overcame Goldberg and successfully defended his World Heavyweight Title.

10 EARLY ENTRY

5.31.2015

Competitors normally enter the arena once their pod opens. However, during the Intercontinental Championship Match in 2015, King Barrett slammed Dolph Ziggler into Mark Henry's pod and shattered the glass, allowing Mark Henry to enter the match early.

1 **STONE COLD STUNNER**
Beginning with a sudden kick to the midsection, Steve Austin's Stone Cold Stunner can end a match at any time.

ATTITUDE ADJUSTMENT **2** ►
John Cena lifts competitors up on his back before throwing them to the mat for an Attitude Adjustment—no matter the size of his opponent.

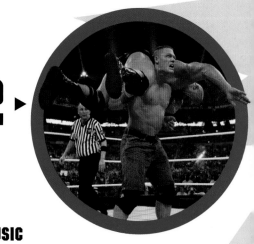

◄ **3** **SWEET CHIN MUSIC**
Shawn Michaels hit his opponents with a powerful jaw-crushing superkick.

RKO **4** ►
Randy Orton traps Superstars in a three-quarter facelock before falling backward and forcing them to the mat.

◄ **5** **PEDIGREE**
Triple H puts his opponents away by hooking both of their arms and driving them into the mat.

DDT **6** ►
Jake "The Snake" Roberts held competitors in an inverted headlock and slammed them into the mat.

◄ **7** **F5**
Brock Lesnar spins opponents over his head before throwing them down in this move, appropriately named after the most destructive category of tornado.

TOP 10 SIGNATURE MOVES

MANY SUPERSTARS USE unique maneuvers to punish the competition. Superstars have adapted and perfected standard ring moves to make them even more devastating and frightening to their opponents.

TOMBSTONE 8▼
Undertaker holds competitors upside down before slamming them to their defeat.

TOP ROPE ELBOW DROP 10▲
Randy Savage put the finishing touches on his opponents by climbing to the top turnbuckle, aiming his elbow at the chest of his foes, and leaping off.

◄9 ## JACKKNIFE POWERBOMB
Diesel was able to win and retain the WWE Championship by lifting his rivals high above his head and then slamming them more than seven feet down to the mat.

TOP 10 WEDDING WOES

THE WWE UNIVERSE HAS seen its share of wedding ceremonies and receptions. When a marriage between Superstars is announced, fireworks are sure to follow. Even if the ceremony goes smoothly, the reception often goes off with a bang.

1 STEPHANIE AND TEST

Things didn't turn out quite as planned for Stephanie McMahon and Test. At the couple's wedding ceremony, Triple H shocked everyone when he revealed that he'd recently married the bride-to-be while she was unconscious, leaving Test and Stephanie unable to tie the knot.

2 RANDY SAVAGE AND MISS ELIZABETH

Randy Savage and Miss Elizabeth's ceremony went off without a hitch. But Jake "The Snake" Roberts ruined the reception by introducing a cobra to the gift pile—which bit the groom!

3 LITA AND KANE

The match between Matt Hardy and Kane at *SummerSlam 2004* stipulated that Hardy's girlfriend, Lita, had to marry the winner. Lita was hoping to marry Hardy, but Hardy lost, and Lita was forced to marry Kane, who was the demonic father of Lita's unborn baby.

4 STEPHANIE MCMAHON AND UNDERTAKER

Undertaker kidnapped the WWE boss's daughter, Stephanie McMahon, during her WWE debut and planned to force her to marry him. Luckily, Stone Cold Steve Austin rescued the bride-to-be from unholy matrimony.

5 BILLY AND CHUCK

Tag team partners Chuck Palumbo and Billy Gunn decided to show their affection for each other in a commitment ceremony. However, the event was interrupted when Eric Bishoff attacked one of the witnesses, Stephanie McMahon. Later, Palumbo and Chuck admitted the union was just a publicity stunt.

6 AL WILSON AND DAWN MARIE

Dawn Marie found a crafty way to get under the skin of her rival Torrie Wilson—she began dating Wilson's aging father, Al. Wilson's rival became her stepmother in January 2003. Tragically, however, Al passed away from a heart attack during the newlyweds' honeymoon.

7 EDGE AND VICKIE GUERRERO

Even though Edge and Vickie's ceremony was uninterrupted, everything went wrong during the reception. Triple H interrupted the event and showed a video of the groom cheating on Vickie with their wedding planner, Alicia Fox.

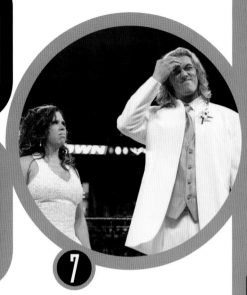

7

8 LANA AND RUSEV

Rusev and Lana did not hold their wedding ceremony in a WWE ring, but they did share the fun of their reception with the WWE Universe. Unfortunately for Lana, a brawl that broke out between her husband, Rusev, and Roman Reigns ended with Lana's face covered in frosting from her wedding cake.

8

9 DAVID FLAIR AND MISS HANCOCK

David Flair and Miss Hancock were expecting a child, and decided to get married. Immediately before the ceremony, Hancock revealed the shocking truth that David was not the father of her child, and the wedding was called off.

10 AJ LEE AND DANIEL BRYAN

AJ Lee was due to marry her on-and-off boyfriend, Daniel Bryan, on the thousandth episode of *RAW*. But Mr. McMahon meddled in the relationship, offering Lee the job of *RAW* General Manager. AJ took the job and left a furious Bryan waiting at the altar.

TOP 10 STARRCADE MOMENTS

THE FLAGSHIP EVENT OF the NWA, and later WCW, was the mighty *Starrcade*. Dubbed "The Grandaddy of Them All," this epic annual supercard saw titles contested by Ric Flair, Lex Luger, and Hulk Hogan, so it's hardly surprising that *Starrcade* produced plenty of unforgettable moments.

1 FLAIR DEFEATS RACE
STARRCADE 1983

Harley Race ended Ric Flair's first NWA Championship reign, then tried to end his career by offering a bounty to anyone who would put him out of action. Flair recovered and beat Race in a Steel Cage Match for the Title at the first-ever *Starrcade*.

2 "I QUIT"
STARRCADE 1985

To settle the rivalry between champion Tully Blanchard and challenger Magnum TA for the United States Championship, the two Superstars agreed to an "I Quit" Match. Magnum TA won after forcing Blanchard to say the humiliating words.

3 A CAREER ON THE LINE
STARRCADE 1993

Returning to WCW after two years in WWE, Ric Flair wanted to regain the WCW Championship. The Champion, Vader, seemed unbeatable, but Flair wagered his career to get a Title shot and managed to reclaim the WCW Championship.

4 THE BLACK SCORPION
STARRCADE 1990

NWA World Heavyweight Champion, Sting, had been dealing with a troublesome masked competitor named the Black Scorpion. The two met in a Steel Cage Match where Sting pinned and unmasked his opponent, revealing his bitter rival, Ric Flair.

5 BATTLEBOWL
STARRCADE 1991

At *BattleBowl* 40 competitors were randomly placed in tag teams, and the winners of 10 matches would meet in a Battle Royal Match to crown the winner. In the Battle Royal, Sting eliminated WCW Champion Lex Luger to win the event overall.

6 THE FAST COUNT
STARRCADE 1997

When the referee made a fast count to aid Hulk Hogan in his **WCW Championship Match** against Sting, Bret Hart imparted justice by restarting the match with himself as referee. Justice prevailed and Sting won.

6

7 DOG COLLAR MATCH
STARRCADE 1983

As well as Harley Race vs. Ric Flair, *Starrcade 1983* also featured a Dog Collar Match between "Rowdy" Roddy Piper and Greg Valentine, who each wore a collar linked by a chain. Piper came out as top dog.

7

8 A WINNING STREAK ENDS
STARRCADE 1998

WCW Champion Goldberg had been unbeaten since his 1997 debut until Kevin Nash challenged him for the Title in a No Disqualification Match at *Starrcade*. Nash pinned Goldberg thanks to Scott Hall, who secretly used a Taser on Goldberg.

10

9 THE WORLD CUP
STARRCADE 1995

WCW and New Japan Pro Wrestling (NJPW) held the World Cup of Wrestling at *Starrcade 1995*. The promotion's Superstars battled to win four matches out of a total seven. Sting beat Kensuke Sasaki in the final match, securing victory for WCW.

10 MADUSA WINS
STARRCADE 1999

Madusa became the first woman to hold the Cruiserweight Title at *Starrcade 1999*. She pinned Evan Karagias in a show of athleticism and secured a place in sports entertainment history.

TOP 10 AMAZING EVENTS

FOR MORE THAN THREE decades, WWE has put together some incredible pay-per-view events and specials. While *WrestleMania*, *SummerSlam*, *Survivor Series*, and *Royal Rumble* are the most notable, many other shows have produced amazing matches and memorable moments.

1 MONEY IN THE BANK 2011
7.17.2011

The night began with two memorable *Money in the Bank* Ladder Matches, won by Daniel Bryan and Alberto Del Rio, but the excitement didn't end there. The partisan Chicago crowd exploded in celebration of CM Punk's WWE Championship victory over John Cena.

2 ECW: ONE NIGHT STAND 2005
6.12.2005

The ECW relaunch began in earnest with this special reunion show that featured dozens of former ECW personalities in a series of matches. In the main event, The Dudley Boyz faced Tommy Dreamer and the Sandman in a tag team event that was eventually won by The Dudley Boyz.

3 UNFORGIVEN 2006
9.17.2006

This packed night included three of the most memorable matches in WWE history. Trish Stratus won her retirement match for the WWE Women's Championship, John Cena took the WWE Title in a Tables, Ladders, and Chairs Match, and D-Generation X (Triple H and Shawn Michaels) won a Handicap Hell in a Cell.

4 INVASION 2001
7.22.2001

The Invasion storyline pitted the best of WWE against the best of the Alliance (a team of ECW and WCW wrestlers) in 11 matches. Heading into the main showdown, a ten-man event called the Inaugural Brawl, each side had won five matches, but the Alliance took the tie-breaking final bout.

5 NO WAY OUT 2001
2.25.2001

On this memorable night, The Rock defeated Kurt Angle for the WWE Championship, leading to a *WrestleMania X-Seven* match with Stone Cold Steve Austin. In the other main event of the night, Steve Austin fell to Triple H in a Three Stages of Hell Match with a score of 2-1.

6 ARMAGEDDON 2000

Five championships were on the line in one night including the WWE European and Intercontinental Championships. The main event saw Kurt Angle defend his WWE Championship in a six-man Hell in a Cell match against Undertaker, The Rock, Triple H, Rikishi, and Stone Cold Steve Austin.

4

STEPHANIE
MCMAHON,
THE
ALLIANCE

"IT'S DO
OR DIE!"

7 EXTREME RULES 2012

After an eight-year absence from WWE rings, "The Beast" Brock Lesnar, returned to face WWE icon John Cena—and lost. The night also featured a WWE Championship Street Fight between CM Punk and Chris Jericho, which ended in CM Punk's victory.

8 BACKLASH 2001

On this night, three championships were on the line in one match. The Two Man Power Trip (Stone Cold Steve Austin and Triple H) defeated the Brothers of Destruction (Undertaker and Kane) in a Winner Takes All Match for the WWE World Tag Team and Intercontinental Championships.

7

9 IN YOUR HOUSE: CANADIAN STAMPEDE 1997

Although the event included a WWE Title Match between Undertaker and Vader and a battle between Triple H and Mankind, the night is remembered for the 10-man match featuring teams captained by Stone Cold Steve Austin and Bret "Hit Man" Hart.

10 KING OF THE RING 1993

This historic show featured WWE's seventh ever *King of the Ring* tournament, an Intercontinental Championship Match between Shawn Michaels, accompanied by Diesel, and Yokozuna challenging Hulk Hogan for the WWE Championship.

TOP 10
DREAM MATCH-UPS

If Superstars from different eras clashed in the ring, who would win?

1 JOHN CENA VS. ANDRE THE GIANT John Cena has always demonstrated incredible strength, and the WWE Universe would love to see if he could lift the mighty Andre the Giant onto his shoulders for an Attitude Adjustment.

2 UNDERTAKER VS. SUPERSTAR BILLY GRAHAM Could the larger-than-life personality of Superstar Billy Graham overcome the fearsome Undertaker?

3 BROCK LESNAR VS. BRUNO SAMMARTINO Both of these Superstars held the WWE Championship and are known for pulverizing strength. Who would be victorious in a match?

4 CHARLOTTE VS. TRISH STRATUS No person won the WWE Women's Championship more often than Trish Stratus, but some fans believe Charlotte might have stopped that from happening.

5 STONE COLD STEVE AUSTIN VS. CM PUNK WWE fans have wanted the unruly Stone Cold Steve Austin to face the equally defiant CM Punk. Which rebel would win?

6 THE HARDY BOYS VS. THE STEINER BROTHERS Each set of brothers dominated tag team competitions during their era.

7 SHAWN MICHAELS VS. DANIEL BRYAN A bout between the Heartbreak Kid and his pupil Daniel Bryan would be amazing. Who would win—the teacher or the student?

8 THE ROCK & ROCKY JOHNSON & HIGH CHIEF PETER MAIVIA VS. THE HART FAMILY The Rock is a third generation Superstar and it would be an awesome battle for him, with his father and grandfather, to face the legendary Hart family.

9 SASHA BANKS VS. LITA A fight between the popular Superstar Sasha Banks and the legendary Lita would be incredible.

10 RANDY ORTON VS. RANDY SAVAGE A pair of second-generation Superstars, which Randy would be victorious?

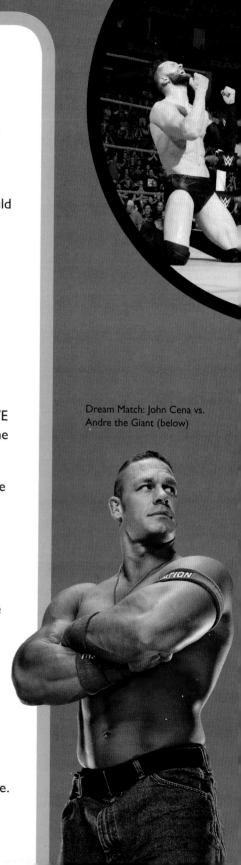

Dream Match: John Cena vs. Andre the Giant (below)

TOP 10
UNEXPECTED WINS

Nothing excites the WWE Universe more than an upset victory.

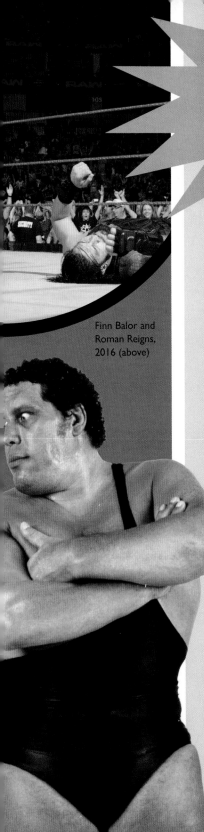

Finn Balor and Roman Reigns, 2016 (above)

1 MAVEN VS. UNDERTAKER [February 7, 2002]
The WWE Universe thought it was a fluke when Maven eliminated Undertaker from the 2002 *Royal Rumble*.

2 MR. MCMAHON AT THE ROYAL RUMBLE [January 24, 1999]
No one expected WWE boss Mr. McMahon to outlast 29 Superstars, but he proved everyone wrong.

3 1-2-3 KID VS. RAZOR RAMON [May 17, 1993] Two weeks after his TV debut, 1-2-3 Kid shockingly defeated Razor Ramon.

4 THE HURRICANE VS. THE ROCK [March 10, 2003]
With Hollywood success going to his head, The Rock did not think The Hurricane could ever defeat him—but he did!

5 JAMES ELLSWORTH VS. AJ STYLES [October 18, 2016]
With help from Dean Ambrose, underdog James Ellsworth upset the WWE World Champion AJ Styles.

6 BARRY HOROWITZ VS. BODYDONNA SKIP
[July 9, 1995] Perennial underachiever Barry Horowitz scored his first WWE win by pinning Bodydonna Skip.

7 JIM ROSS VS. TRIPLE H [April 18, 2005]
Legendary commentator Ross found himself in a match with Triple H. Ross won with Batista's help.

8 FINN BALOR VS. ROMAN REIGNS [July 25, 2016] Newcomer Bálor won against former WWE World Champion, Reigns.

9 THE BLUE MEANIE VS. JBL [July 7, 2005] The Blue Meanie scored a shocking victory against the veteran JBL.

10 RICK RUDE VS. THE ULTIMATE WARRIOR [April 2, 1989]
The Ultimate Warrior was the Intercontinental Heavyweight Champion, but Rick Rude claimed it by pinning him down.

TOP 10 GREATEST MANAGERS

A GREAT MANAGER CAN take a Superstar's career to the next level by focusing their charge and helping him or her earn championship opportunities and main-event matches. With the right manager a struggling performer can become a future Hall of Famer.

1 BOBBY HEENAN

Numerous Hall of Famers have been members of the Heenan Family, including Nick Bockwinkel, Harley Race, Ric Flair, and Mr. Perfect. Bobby Heenan guided Andre the Giant in his *WrestleMania III* bout against Hulk Hogan.

2 JJ DILLON

Best known for leading the infamous Four Horsemen faction, JJ Dillon was the most successful manager in NWA and WCW history. He guided Ric Flair, Arn Anderson, Ole Anderson, Tully Blanchard, Lex Luger, and Barry Windham to multiple singles and tag team championships.

3 SENSATIONAL SHERRI

After a successful career as a Superstar, Sensational Sherri brought her commanding in-ring personality to the role of manager. She managed Superstars Buddy Rose and Doug Somers to the AWA Tag Team Championship, but Sherri is most famous for guiding Randy Savage and Shawn Michaels to glory in WWE.

4 PAUL HEYMAN

After leading the Dangerous Alliance stable in AWA, WCW, and ECW as "Paul E. Dangerously," Paul Heyman took a leadership role in ECW. After its closure, Heyman joined WWE, and managed CM Punk during his epic title reign, Brock Lesnar's explosive return, and many others.

5 PAUL BEARER

A few months after Undertaker debuted in WWE, Paul Bearer joined the menacing Superstar as his manager. Undertaker won his first WWE Championship later that year. Paul Bearer also famously introduced Undertaker's estranged brother, Kane, to WWE.

6 MR. FUJI

Mr. Fuji started his career as a competitor, winning the WWE Tag Team Championship five times. His championship pedigree enabled him to guide the tag team Demolition to championship gold. Mr. Fuji also managed famed Superstar Yokozuna who went on to gain two WWE Championships.

7 MISS ELIZABETH

In 1985, Savage shocked several potential suitors when he hired the elegant Miss Elizabeth. Randy's decision proved incredibly successful inside the ring and out. The two married at *SummerSlam 1991* in what was called "The Match Made in Heaven."

8 JIMMY HART

"The Mouth of the South" Jimmy Hart used his megaphone to shout encouragement at his clients, and insults at their competitors. He guided many teams to World Tag Team Championship runs and steered the Honky Tonk Man to the longest ever Intercontinental Championship reign.

9 FREDDIE BLASSIE

As his manager, Freddie Blassie led the villainous Superstar Iron Shiek to the WWE Championship in late 1983. He then guided the Iron Shiek and Nikolai Volkoff to the Tag Team Championship at the inaugural *WrestleMania* in 1985.

10 CAPTAIN LOU ALBANO

The most successful manager of tag team competitors in history, Captain Lou Albano guided his charges to 17 reigns as Tag Team Champions. He also managed Ivan Koloff when he ended Bruno Sammartino's record-setting seven-year reign as WWE Champion.

JIMMY HART

"WE ARE COOL ... AND WE ARE CONFIDENT!"

143

TOP 10 FANTASTIC FINALES

MATCHES ALWAYS KEEP the WWE Universe biting their nails because the outcome is far from certain. Anything can happen—a match-finishing move can come out of nowhere suddenly ending a bout, or a pinned Superstar can fight their way out of a count out, leading to a shocking and unexpected reversal.

1 — 3.29.2015
BROCK LESNAR VS. ROMAN REIGNS

WrestleMania 31 saw a clash between Brock Lesnar and Roman Reigns. But the match was turned around when Seth Rollins cashed in his *Money in the Bank* title opportunity and won the match and the WWE World Heavyweight Championship.

2 — 3.31.1996
SHAWN MICHAELS VS. BRET "HIT MAN" HART

After the full hour of a 60-Minute Iron Man Match for the WWE Championship at *WrestleMania XII*, no decision had been scored. Just one minute and 52 seconds into overtime, Michaels stunned Hart with a superkick to his chin, ending the match.

3 — 1.22.1994
ROYAL RUMBLE 1994

30 Superstars competed for a chance to win the WWE Championship at *WrestleMania*. Competitor after competitor was thrown from the ring, losing their shot at winning until just Bret Hart and Lex Luger remained. Both went over the ropes together, producing the first tie in *Royal Rumble* history.

4 — 4.6.2014
BROCK LESNAR VS. UNDERTAKER

After 21 consecutive *WrestleMania* victories, no one thought Undertaker could be beaten. After 25 minutes and 12 seconds at *WrestleMania 30*, Lesnar hoisted Undertaker up and spun into an F-5, slamming him down and pinning him to end Undertaker's streak.

5 — 9.27.1998
STONE COLD STEVE AUSTIN VS. UNDERTAKER VS. KANE

Undertaker and Kane challenged Austin for the WWE Championship. The two grabbed Austin and slammed him to the mat before pinning him, but no new winner was announced. WWE boss Mr. McMahon fled the arena with the Title!

6 SHAWN MICHAELS VS. RIC FLAIR

3.30.2008

Shawn Michaels faced ring legend Ric Flair in the final match of Flair's storied career. A torn Michaels mouthed "I'm sorry, I love you" to Flair before delivering a trademark superkick to Flair's chin, pinning him and ending his career.

7 STONE COLD STEVE AUSTIN VS. MR. MCMAHON & BIG SHOW

2.14.1999

Mr. McMahon faced Austin in a Steel Cage Match to prevent him from making it to *WrestleMania XV*. But a Big Show entered the cage through a hole in the canvas, throwing Austin and breaking the cage. Austin won because he was the first to escape.

8 JOHN CENA VS. BATISTA

4.25.2010

Cena and Batista fought in a gruelling Last Man Standing Match, which saw the Superstars trade brutal blows. To ensure his victory, Cena threw Batista to the ground and duct-taped him to the ringpost facedown so Batista could not get up during the countout.

9 FANDANGO VS. CHRIS JERICHO

4.7.2013

When Fandango debuted at *WrestleMania 29*, no one thought the ballroom dancer stood a chance against six-time World Champion Chris Jericho. But Jericho tweaked his knee during the match, allowing Fandango to free himself from Jericho's near-match-winning hold and pin Jericho for a shocking win.

10 ROYAL RUMBLE 2000

1.23.2000

The Rock and Big Show battled to win the *Royal Rumble* match, which also gave the winner a chance to compete at *WrestleMania*. In the final moments, Big Show attempted to throw The Rock from the ring but instead tipped over the ropes and lost the match.

TOP 10s

CHAMPIONSHIPS AND LEGENDS

TOP 10
UNITED STATES CHAMPIONS

THE UNITED STATES Championship began in WCW in 1974. Later, it would be defended on *RAW* and *SmackDown*. Over the years, many of the greatest names in sports entertainment have held the coveted United States Championship Title.

1 LEX LUGER

A five-time Champion, Lex Luger's 17-month reign from May 1989 to October 1990 is the single longest run in the Title's history. Luger lived up to his "Total Package" nickname by dominating his rivals with the Torture Rack, a move that displayed his incredible power.

2 RIC FLAIR

In addition to being a 16-time World Champion, Ric Flair also holds the record for United States Championship reigns at six wins. Flair has held the Title in three different decades, and has defeated an eclectic range of Champions, including Mr. Wrestling, Ricky Steamboat, and Bobo Brazil.

3 WAHOO MCDANIEL

From August 1981 through to March 1985, Wahoo McDaniel held the United States Championship on five separate occasions. McDaniel engaged in a lengthy rivalry with Sgt. Slaughter for the Title, with the two trading the Championship four times.

4 "RAVISHING" RICK RUDE

"Ravishing" Rick Rude made his one run with the United States Championship really count. Facing an injured Sting at *Clash of the Champions XVII*, Rude put up a hearty fight and was able to win the Championship. Rude then began a lengthy reign with the Title, holding on to it for well over a year.

5 BLACKJACK MULLIGAN

Mulligan was the first man to win the United States Championship three times. The brash Texan successfully defended his Title by using his favorite finishing move, the Clawhold, to grip the heads of his opponents, forcing them to submit.

6 HARLEY RACE

Winning a tournament for the new United States Championship in 1975, Harley Race became the first man to ever be crowned Champion. He held the patriotic Title for six months before losing it to Johnny Valentine in July 1975.

7 MAGNUM TA

Magnum TA held the United States Championship twice, for a total of 10 months. He ended Wahoo McDaniel's final Championship reign, and later won a vicious "I Quit" Match against Tully Blanchard. But Magnum suffered career-shortening injuries in a car accident.

8

8 BOOKER T

A four-time United States Champion, Booker T is one of the few Superstars to hold the United States Championship in WCW and WWE. Booker T won the Title at WCW's _Greed_ pay-per-view event in 2001, and still held the Title when WWE purchased WCW. He then won the Title three more times.

4

9 JOHN CENA

In 2003, the Championship was revived after a brief retirement. Since then, no one has won the Title more times than John Cena. His first reign came at the expense of Big Show at _WrestleMania XX_. Cena then won the Title an astounding four more times, and stirred controversy with his spinning belt.

10 GOLDBERG

Goldberg held the Title for just two months, but his reign did not end by defeat. In the midst of his historic 173-0 winning streak, Goldberg forfeited the Championship when he overcame the villainous Hulk Hogan for the WCW World Heavyweight Championship.

TOP 10 SUPERSTARS NEVER TO WIN THE WWE CHAMPIONSHIP

THE WWE CHAMPIONSHIP IS "THE richest prize" in sports entertainment. Winning it is a goal for any Superstar who steps into the ring. Still, some Superstars who never held this prize are widely acclaimed for their other great achievements.

Roddy Piper hoped to win a WWE Championship.

Unfortunately, Dusty Rhodes never managed to win the WWE Championship.

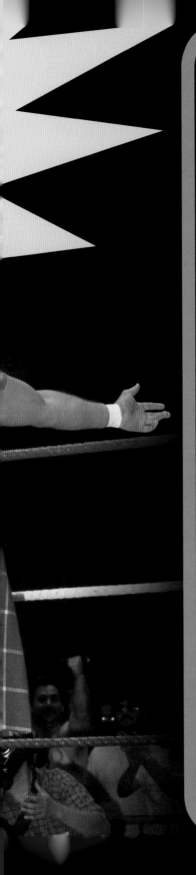

1 DUSTY RHODES

Rhodes won several Heavyweight Championships during his 48-year long career, but he never managed to capture the WWE Championship.

2 RICKY "THE DRAGON" STEAMBOAT

Steamboat was a strong Intercontinental Champion, but never had the chance to challenge for the WWE Title.

3 JAKE "THE SNAKE" ROBERTS

Roberts terrorized several WWE Champions including Hulk Hogan, but he never captured the Title himself.

4 RODDY PIPER

While WWE Champion Hulk Hogan experienced a surge of popularity in the 1980s, Piper was the main antagonist looking to end his reign at the top.

5 THE BRITISH BULLDOG

Bulldog boasted reigns with the Intercontinental, European, and Tag Team Championships but fell short of winning the WWE Title.

6 KING KONG BUNDY

Massive Bundy fought for the WWE Championship at *WrestleMania 2*, but he was defeated by Hulk Hogan.

7 OWEN HART

Owen had the ability to win the WWE Title and nearly took it from his brother, Bret Hart, at *SummerSlam 1994*.

8 MR. PERFECT

Although Mr. Perfect lived up to his moniker, he was never able to showcase his talent to win the WWE Title.

9 RON SIMMONS

He was the first African American WCW Champion, but he never won the WWE Title.

10 HARLEY RACE

The eight-time NWA Heavyweight Champion could never win the greatest prize of them all.

TOP 10

WCW WORLD HEAVYWEIGHT CHAMPIONS

FROM 1991 THROUGH 2001, the WCW World Heavyweight Championship was the biggest prize in WCW. This hugely prestigious title has been held by 22 men, including all-time greats and some of the most controversial world champions in the history of sports entertainment.

1 RIC FLAIR

In 1991, Ric Flair was the first to hold the Title of WCW World Heavyweight Champion. During his career in WCW (1991 and 1993–2001), he won the Title a record seven times, defeating competitors including Vader, Hulk Hogan, and Randy Savage.

2 STING

Whether sporting spiky blond hair or a black trench coat, Sting was always a contender for the WCW World Heavyweight Championship, and won the Title six times. He defeated Lex Luger for his first Title, but his most exciting Championship victory was in 1997, when he dethroned the legendary Hulk Hogan.

3 HULK HOGAN

In 1994, Hulk Hogan joined WCW. He made an immediate impact, beating Ric Flair for the WCW World Heavyweight Title in his debut match. Hogan held the Title for more than 15 months—the longest WCW Title reign in its history—and held onto his second Championship for almost a year.

4 VADER

One of the most intimidating competitors in sports entertainment history, Vader first claimed the WCW World Heavyweight Championship against Sting at *The Great American Bash* in 1992. Each of his three reigns was longer than the previous one, but his run of victories ended at *Starrcade* in 1993.

5 BOOKER T

WCW World Television Champion and United States Champion Booker T's biggest victory came on July 9, 2000, when he beat Jeff Jarrett for the WCW World Heavyweight Title. Over the next 12 months, he famously became a five-time WCW Champion.

6 GOLDBERG

In 1997, Goldberg joined WCW. He won his first match in September and by July 1998 he had to face WCW Champion "Hollywood" Hulk Hogan. Goldberg beat the legend for the Title. The wins continued until December 1998, when Kevin Nash took the Title and ended Goldberg's streak.

①

7 LEX LUGER

In July 1991, Lex Luger defeated Barry Windham in a steel cage and took the WCW Title. Luger held the Championship for more than seven months before losing it to Sting. Five years later, Luger beat Hulk Hogan for the Title—clinching his second Championship.

8 KEVIN NASH

In December 1998, Kevin Nash halted Goldberg's winning streak to take the WCW World Heavyweight Championship with the help of his tag team partner, Scott Hall. The next week, Nash let "Hollywood" Hulk Hogan pin him, handing the Title to Hogan. Nash went on to win the Title a further four times.

⑤

9 THE GIANT

When Big Show began his career in WCW, he took on the name The Giant. At 7-feet tall, he towered over competitors and became one of the youngest World Champions, aged 23, when he defeated Hulk Hogan. The Giant won the Championship again the next year and held it for more than three months.

10 RON SIMMONS

In 1992, Ron Simmons, the former All-American Florida State football player, took the WCW World Heavyweight Championship title from reigning champion Vader. Simmons held the Title for an impressive five months before losing it back to Vader.

2

WWE COMMENTATOR

"YOU GOTTA BE KIDDING ME!"

1 DAVID ARQUETTE

For 12 days in 2000, the WCW World Heavyweight Championship was held by actor David Arquette. Teaming with Jeff Jarrett, this unlikely champion earned his victory by pinning WCW executive Eric Bischoff instead of the champion, Diamond Dallas Page.

2 MR. MCMAHON

Although he doesn't normally compete, WWE Chairman Mr. McMahon managed to win two championships. Stone Cold Steve Austin helped him win the WWE Championship in 1999, and in 2007 McMahon won the ECW World Heavyweight Championship in a 3-on-1 Handicap Match.

3 HERVINA

Male Superstar Harvey Wippleman won the WWE Women's Championship dressed as a woman known as Hervina. He pinned the WWE Women's Champion, The Kat, before whipping off his wig and revealing his identity. Just one day later, Jacqueline took Hervina's Title in under a minute.

4 HULK HOGAN

When challenging his fellow nWo teammate, Kevin Nash, for the WCW World Heavyweight Championship Title, Hulk Hogan poked Nash in the chest. Nash fell to the mat, allowing himself to be pinned by Hogan to give Hogan the Championship. It became known as the "Fingerpoke of Doom."

5 JUDY BAGWELL

After Buff Bagwell and his tag team partner Rick Steiner split up, Steiner teamed up with Bagwell's 50-year-old mother, Judy Bagwell, in a controversial mixed-gender pairing. Judy Bagwell became the only female to hold one half of the WCW Tag Team Championship.

6 MIDEON

Shane McMahon successfully defended the European Championship at *WrestleMania XV*, but retired it shortly afterward. Three months later, Mideon found the European Championship in Shane's duffle bag. Shane allowed Mideon to keep the Title and crown himself European Champion.

7 OKLAHOMA

Oklahoma annoyed fans when he mocked beloved WWE announcer Jim Ross. He caused further discord when he stole the WCW Cruiserweight Championship by defeating Madusa at *Souled Out 2000*. Oklahoma vacated the Title a few days later.

8 JIM DUGGAN

Scott Hall won the WCW Television Championship, but in an act of disrespect, he tossed the Title in the garbage. Janitor Jim Duggan fished it out of the trash and proclaimed himself the new WCW Television Champion.

9 STEPHANIE MCMAHON

Not everyone liked the boss's daughter, Stephanie McMahon, but the infrequent competitor had some friends fighting in her corner. Superstars X-Pac and Tori helped Stephanie McMahon win the WWE Women's Championship in March 2000. She managed to hold the Title for five months.

10 BRET "HIT MAN" HART

In 2010, returning after a 12-year hiatus, Bret Hart succeeded not only in making peace with WWE but also in winning his fifth United States Championship from The Miz. It was Hart's first title in WWE since 1997, despite no longer actively competing.

SOME CHAMPIONSHIP winners seem less deserving than others. Controversial Superstars both delight and dismay the WWE Universe. Their reigns tend to be short-lived. It's only a matter of time before a less divisive competitor steps forward to claim the title—and restore order in and out of the ring.

TOP 10 HARDCORE CHAMPIONS

IN 1998, WWE BOSS Mr. McMahon gave loyal competitor Mankind a Championship to honor him for his unique and brutal style of competition. The title later became known as the Hardcore Championship and was active until 2002.

1 CRASH HOLLY

Crash Holly created the 24/7 rule, meaning that any Superstar could challenge for the Hardcore title at any time and in any place as long as there was a referee present to call the match. Crash Holly took advantage of the rule to capture the title 22 times over the four years the title existed.

2 MICK FOLEY

Mr. McMahon personally crowned Mick Foley the first-ever Hardcore Champion. Foley held the title just once for almost a month before he lost it to The Big Boss Man in a Ladder Match. But the Hardcore Legend is still the embodiment of what the title stands for.

3 STEVE BLACKMAN

Steve Blackman held the WWE Hardcore Championship just six times. However, the cumulative days of his reigns totaled almost six months, meaning Blackman holds the record for most days as WWE Hardcore Champion.

4 RAVEN

With the 24/7 rule in place, the Hardcore Championship title changed hands frequently, and some Superstars racked up high numbers of reigns. Raven won the championship an astonishing 27 times between 2000 and 2002.

5 BIG BOSS MAN

The Big Boss Man was the second Superstar to ever hold the WWE Hardcore Championship, and the first Superstar to win the title four times. His final reign of 97 days—between October 12, 1999 and January 17, 2000—was the longest uninterrupted run in the Championship's history.

6 STEVEN RICHARDS

Steven Richards held the WWE Hardcore Championship on 21 different occasions, but due to the 24/7 rule, just one of those reigns was longer than a week. He won his first WWE Hardcore Championship from Tommy Dreamer and poetically lost his final Hardcore title to Dreamer, too.

7 ROB VAN DAM

The extreme Superstar Rob Van Dam was a four-time WWE Hardcore Champion. Van Dam beat Tommy Dreamer to unify two titles: the Hardcore Championship and the Intercontinental Championship. Van Dam is in the record books as the final Hardcore Champion.

RAVEN

"I WANT ELIMINATION BY ANY MEANS NECESSARY."

8 TERRY FUNK

Terry Funk was a hardcore wrestling pioneer and began fighting in rings roped off with barbed wire before any Hardcore Championship titles existed. After WCW founded its own Hardcore Championship in 1999, Funk won the title three times before it was retired in 2001.

4

9 AL SNOW

A close friend of Mick Foley, Al Snow captured the WWE Hardcore Championship six times and held the title for 129 days. That total is only exceeded by three competitors in the history of the championship.

10 NORMAN SMILEY

Norman Smiley was the first competitor to win the WCW Hardcore Championship. He won the title on November 21, 1999 and held it for almost two months—the longest reign in the title's history—before he lost the title to Brian Knobbs in January 2000.

TOP 10 SURPRISING CHAMPIONS

HEADING INTO A MATCH, there is often a clear favorite—but favorites are not certainties. Sometimes a Superstar bucks the odds and defeats an opponent they were not expected to. That's enough of a shock to the WWE Universe, but it's even more of a shock when one of these upsets leads to a championship title.

1 SHAWN STASIAK
08.18.2002

Perhaps no Superstar suffered more from the Hardcore Championship's 24/7 rule—stating the Title must be defended at all times—than Stasiak. He won the Title 15 times, but never left an arena with the Championship, meaning his collective time as Champion amounted to less than eight hours.

2 IVAN KOLOFF
01.18.1971

For almost eight years, Bruno Sammartino was the WWE Champion. The WWE Universe was confident that a match with Ivan Koloff would be another successful defense. But Koloff stunned everyone by pulling off an improbable victory to become the third WWE Champion in history.

3 THE FABULOUS MOOLAH
10.17.1999

The Fabulous Moolah is widely regarded as one of the greatest Women's Champions of all time. After 40 years in the ring, she seemed to finally call it a day in the late 1980s. But in 1999, the Fabulous Moolah shocked the WWE Universe by roaring back to begin her final reign at the age of 76.

4 GILLBERG
11.17.1998

Duane Gill, a Superstar with a track record of losing more matches than he won, gained notoriety when he transformed himself into Gillberg, a parody of Goldberg. The change did him good. During his time as Gillberg, this ex-failure held the Light Heavyweight Title for a record 15 months.

5 THE ROCK & UNDERTAKER
12.18.2000

Some surprises are down to unexpected team-ups rather than unexpected victories. While The Rock and Undertaker were bitter rivals for most of their careers, they briefly put their animosity aside to beat Edge and Christian for the World Tag Championship, a one-day Title reign.

6 VICKIE GUERRERO

05.18.2009

The title of Miss *WrestleMania* was earned by Santina Marella at *WrestleMania 25*, but "she" lost the moniker to a shock victor in a May 2009 episode of *RAW*. That victor was Vickie Guerrero, General Manager of *RAW* and far from a typical WWE Superstar.

7 MIKEY WHIPWRECK

10.28.1995

In the biggest underdog story in ECW history, Mikey Whipwreck pinned Sandman to win the ECW Championship in October 1995. Prior to his Championship win, Whipwreck was more used to taking punishment than dealing it.

8 OWEN HART

01.20.1998

Owen Hart thought he'd be facing Triple H for the European Championship. Instead, he found himself facing Goldust dressed to impersonate him. Much to Triple H's chagrin, the WWE Commissioner allowed the Title to change hands when Owen beat the faux champion.

9 VINCE RUSSO

09.25.2000

Although not a Superstar, pundit Vince Russo challenged Booker T for the WCW Championship in a Steel Cage Match. Amazingly, Russo managed to earn himself a victory, albeit a tainted one. Goldberg speared Russo through the cage wall, causing him to drop to the floor and thus claim the win.

10 FRITZ VON ERICH

06.14.1982

Just a few months shy of his 53rd birthday, Dallas icon Fritz Von Erich entered the ring for his retirement match. Von Erich shocked the wrestling world and showed everyone he still had it by beating 27-year-old King Kong Bundy for the WCCW Championship.

TOP 10 INTERCONTINENTAL CHAMPIONS

FOR MORE THAN 35 YEARS, the Intercontinental Championship has been a coveted title in WWE. Starting with the inaugural Champ, Pat Patterson, it boasts a lineage of titleholders that reads like a Hall of Fame rollcall, with many of its Superstars reaching greater heights—thanks to their world-class title reigns.

Shelton Benjamin at *Taboo Tuesday*, 10.19.2004

The Miz showing off the Intercontinental Title on *SmackDown Live* in 2016.

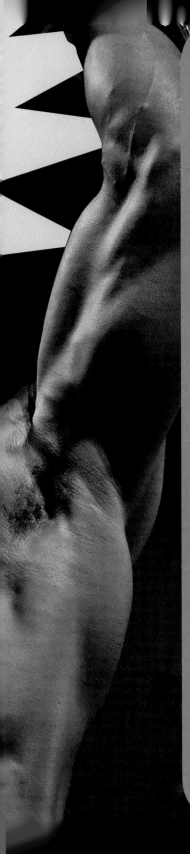

1 CHRIS JERICHO

Between December 1999 and 2009, Jericho held the Intercontinental Championship a record nine times.

2 THE HONKY TONK MAN

The Honky Tonk Man's sole reign lasted 454 days, a record that has stood for almost 30 years.

3 DON MURACO

Muraco traded the Intercontinental Championship with Pedro Morales for three turbulent years in the early 1980s.

4 TITO SANTANA

Tito Santana twice won the Intercontinental Championship, holding it for a total of 14 months.

5 RANDY SAVAGE

Savage held the Title for almost 14 months in the 1980s, twice defending it in classic *WrestleMania* matches.

6 THE MIZ

The Miz has held the Intercontinental Championship six times. His fifth reign, at six months, was the longest.

7 SHELTON BENJAMIN

A pure athlete, Benjamin's first reign began after the WWE Universe selected him to challenge Chris Jericho.

8 ULTIMATE WARRIOR

The Ultimate Warrior defeated the Honky Tonk Man in just 30 seconds to win his first Championship.

9 MR. PERFECT

Mr. Perfect saw his 13-month reign ended by the Texas Tornado at *SummerSlam 1990*, but came storming back to retake the Championship in November 1990.

10 RAZOR RAMON

Ramon held the Title four times between 1993 and 1996, his reigns marked by a rivalry with Shawn Michaels.

TOP 10 LONGEST CHAMPIONSHIP REIGNS

THE LONGER A CHAMP holds onto a title, the more of an achievement it is to be the one to dethrone them. In recent times, title reigns lasting more than a year have become rare, meaning that some of the older, longer records are unlikely to be beaten.

1 — 28 years

THE FABULOUS MOOLAH
WOMEN'S CHAMPIONSHIP

No Superstar has held a championship as long as the Fabulous Moolah. She won the Women's Championship title in 1956 before losing it to Wendi Richter in 1984.

2 — 7 years, 8 months

BRUNO SAMMARTINO
WWE CHAMPIONSHIP

Less than a month after WWE crowned Buddy Rogers as its first ever World Champion in 1963, Bruno Sammartino defeated the champion for the title in just 48 seconds. Sammartino then held the Championship for almost eight years.

3 — 7 years, 3 months

VERNE GAGNE
AWA CHAMPIONSHIP

Gagne held the AWA Championship 10 times between 1960 and 1981. During his ninth and longest AWA Championship reign, Gagne held the Title from August 31, 1968 to November 8, 1975, before Gagne lost the title to Nick Bockwinkel.

4 — 2 years, 6 months

TED DIBIASE
THE MILLION DOLLAR CHAMPIONSHIP

After failing to win the WWE Championship, a frustrated Ted DiBiase created the Million Dollar Championship for himself in 1989. DiBiase held the Title for two-and-a-half years, before he lost it to his former servant, Virgil.

5 — 2 years, 5 months

THE GLAMOUR GIRLS
WOMEN'S TAG TEAM CHAMPIONSHIP

Tag Team partners Judy Martin and Leilani Kai, known as the Glamour Girls, held the Women's Tag Team Championship twice in the five years the Title existed. The Glamour Girls held the Title for 29 months after their first win in 1985.

6 — LEX LUGER
UNITED STATES CHAMPIONSHIP

1 year, 5 months

Luger had the longest reign in the history of the United States Championship. First winning the Title in May 1989, he lost it to Stan Hansen at *Halloween Havoc* in 1990, but regained the Title just two months later and held it for another seven months.

7 — THE NEW DAY
WORLD TAG TEAM CHAMPIONSHIP

1 year, 4 months

Tag team partners Kofi Kingston, Big E and Xavier Woods, collectively known as The New Day, won their second WWE Tag Team Championship at *SummerSlam 2015*. They didn't relinquish the titles until *Roadblock: End of the Line* in April 2016.

8 — HULK HOGAN
WCW CHAMPIONSHIP

1 year, 3 months

Hulk Hogan has the distinction of being the longest reigning WCW Champion in the Title's history. He won the Title in his WCW debut at *Bash at the Beach* in July 1994, but lost it to The Giant at *Halloween Havoc 1995*.

9 — THE HONKY TONK MAN
INTERCONTINENTAL CHAMPIONSHIP

1 year, 2 months

After the Honky Tonk Man defeated Ricky "The Dragon" Steamboat in a June 1987 Intercontinental Championship Match, it took 14 months until he lost the Title to the Ultimate Warrior at *SummerSlam 1988*.

10 — SHANE DOUGLAS
ECW CHAMPIONSHIP

1 year, 2 months

Douglas held the ECW Championship four times between September 1993 and December 1996. His longest reign lasted from November 1997 to January 1999, when he lost the title to Tazz at *Guilty as Charged*.

TOP 10

SHORTEST CHAMPIONSHIP REIGNS

BECOMING A CHAMPION is hard, and holding onto a championship title is even more difficult. The reign of a champion can come to an end in a matter of minutes, hours, or days. Sometimes, it takes just a fraction of the time it took to win to lose everything.

1 — 10.12.2009

JILLIAN HALL
DIVAS CHAMPIONSHIP (5 MINUTES)

Jillian Hall won her first (and only) Divas Championship on an October 2009 episode of *RAW*. She was forced to immediately defend it to *RAW*'s newest acquisition Melina, and she quickly became a former champion.

2 — 4.4.1993

YOKOZUNA
WWE CHAMPIONSHIP (10 MINUTES)

Yokozuna won the WWE Championship from Bret "Hit Man" Hart at *WrestleMania IX*. Right after his win, Yokozuna's manager, Mr. Fuji, challenged Hulk Hogan to a match only to see his client lose the Championship.

3 — 12.18.2011

BIG SHOW
WORLD HEAVYWEIGHT CHAMPIONSHIP (10 MINUTES)

After winning the World Heavyweight Title from Mark Henry, Big Show was forced to immediately defend it against *Money in the Bank* winner Daniel Bryan, who ended Show's reign in minutes.

4 — 4.22.2000

TOMMY DREAMER
ECW CHAMPIONSHIP (15 MINUTES)

Tommy Dreamer finally won the ECW Championship at *CyberSlam 2000* after trying to win the Title for seven years. But Justin Credible beat him in an impromptu match that immediately followed.

5 — 10.22.1995

DEAN DOUGLAS
INTERCONTINENTAL CHAMPIONSHIP (15 MINUTES)

Dean Douglas won the Title when Shawn Michaels had to forfeit it due to injury. However, right after winning it, Douglas had to defend it against Razor Ramon—and lost.

6 MICKIE JAMES
WWE WOMEN'S CHAMPIONSHIP
(1 HOUR)

4.24.2007

Mickie James won the Title, but Mr. McMahon's Executive Assistant, Jonathan Coachman, demanded an immediate rematch. The former champion Melina reclaimed her Title within an hour.

7 EDGE & CHRISTIAN
WORLD TAG TEAM CHAMPIONSHIP
(1 HOUR)

3.19.2001

When travel chaos forced the Dudley Boyz to miss their title shot, Edge and Christian stepped in and won. The Dudleys got the opportunity to battle later that night and took the Championship.

8 STING
WCW CHAMPIONSHIP (2 HOURS)

4.26.1999

Sting was a six-time WCW Championship winner. However, his fifth reign was not exactly a success. While he defeated Diamond Dallas Page to win the Title, he lost it back to Page again the same night in a Fatal 4-Way Match.

9 JOHN CENA & THE MIZ
WWE TAG TEAM CHAMPIONSHIP
(2 HOURS)

4.3.2011

Cena and The Miz defeated villainous stable The Corre for the WWE Tag Team Championship. On the same night, Cena and The Miz lost to the Corre in a rematch and had to give up the Title.

10 FINN BALOR
WWE UNIVERSAL CHAMPIONSHIP
(LESS THAN ONE DAY)

8.21.2016

RAW rookie Finn Balor faced two-time WWE Champion Seth Rollins. Balor won, but he injured his shoulder during the match and surrendered the Title the next night.

1 TRIPLE H

Triple H was the first-ever Superstar to hold the World Heavyweight Championship in WWE. He fought a wide variety of challengers, including Shawn Michaels, Booker T, Goldberg, Scott Steiner, Rob Van Dam, and Randy Orton for the Title, which he held five times between 2002 and 2005.

2 EDGE

With seven separate reigns, Edge has held the World Heavyweight Championship more times than any other Superstar in WWE history. His seventh and final reign came to an end in 2011 when injuries forced him to retire from the ring and vacate the World Heavyweight Championship.

3 BATISTA

Batista first won his World Heavyweight Championship in 2005 and held it for a record 282 days, a reign which only ended because an injury forced him to relinquish the Championship. Batista captured it within four months of his return to the ring, and went on to win it two more times.

4 SHEAMUS

Sheamus was a one-time World Heavyweight Champion, winning the Title at *WrestleMania XXVIII* by pinning champion at the time Daniel Bryan in an astonishing 18 seconds. The Celtic Warrior held the Title for almost seven months—the third longest reign in the Title's history.

5 CM PUNK

The Straight Edge Superstar was the first competitor to win *Money in the Bank* twice, giving him the opportunity to cash in both wins to compete for any championship he wanted. Both times, Punk chose the World Heavyweight Championship, and both times, Punk won.

6 UNDERTAKER

Undertaker won the World Heavyweight Championship three times—twice in *WrestleMania* matches. He defeated Batista at *WrestleMania 23* to win his first World Heavyweight Championship, and the following year he pinned Edge at *WrestleMania XXIV* to capture the Title for a second time.

7 KANE

In May 2010, Kane won a Money in the Bank Ladder Match, which guaranteed him a championship opportunity. Kane became the first Superstar to cash in his chance on the same night, defeating Rey Mysterio to win the World Heavyweight Title. He held the Title for five months.

8 RANDY ORTON

When Orton won the World Heavyweight Championship aged 24 at *SummerSlam 2004* he was the youngest world champion in WWE history. He also became the last World Heavyweight Champion at *TLC 2013* when he pinned John Cena to unify the Title with the WWE Championship.

9 JOHN CENA

John Cena won the World Heavyweight Championship three times. Cena first won the Title at *Survivor Series 2008* in a particularly special moment. Having returned from an injury that had sidelined him for months, he won the Title in front of his hometown fans in Boston, Massachusetts.

10 REY MYSTERIO

Known as the Ultimate Underdog, Rey Mysterio often faced a significant size disadvantage when he competed for the World Heavyweight Championship. However, Mysterio twice managed to overcome the odds and win the World Heavyweight Title.

THERE WERE 56 World Heavyweight Championship title holders between its introduction to WWE in 2002 and December 2013, when it was unified with the WWE Championship. But only a handful of winners stick in the WWE Universe's memory as the greatest Heavyweight Champions.

TOP 10 FEMALE CHAMPIONS

WOMEN HAVE COMPETED in WWE for more than five decades, and some of the most popular female Superstars have held the Championship, including multiple WWE Hall of Famers. These pioneers blazed a trail for a new generation of female Superstars.

1 THE FABULOUS MOOLAH

The Fabulous Moolah won the Women's Championship in 1956 and held the Title for the next 28 years. She was the first woman inducted into the WWE Hall of Fame and she continued to compete into her 80s. Moolah held the Title four times during her career.

2 TRISH STRATUS

When Trish Stratus first joined WWE in 2000, she was a manager, not an in-ring competitor. However, she surprised everyone by winning the Women's Championship a record seven times. Her final Title victory came in her retirement match at *Unforgiven 2006*.

3 MEDUSA

Medusa held AWA's World Women's Championship for almost a year, and held the Women's Championship three times in the 1990s when she competed under the name Alundra Blayze. She then jumped to WCW and became the first woman to win the WCW Cruiserweight Championship.

4 CHYNA

Chyna won the Women's Championship against the villainous Superstar, Ivory, at *WrestleMania X-Seven*. She went on to crush all challengers for the Title over the next seven months until she left WWE and retired from sports entertainment.

5 LITA

Beating the boss might not be the best move for continued job security, but that's exactly what Lita did when she defeated Stephanie McMahon for the Women's Championship in August 2000. Lita went on to win the Championship three more times.

6 MICKIE JAMES

Only a handful of women have held both the WWE Women's Championship and the WWE Divas Championship, and Mickie James is perhaps the most decorated Superstar to do so. James held the WWE Women's Championship five times.

7 NIKKI BELLA

AJ Lee's reign as WWE Diva's Champion was ended by Nikki Bella, who then outlasted Lee's 295-day title reign by six days. But Nikki's long run wasn't achieved alone—her twin sister, Brie, aided her by confusing officials and competitors.

8 AJ LEE

From June 2013 to November 2014, AJ Lee was the dominant figure in the WWE Divas Division. Over that period, Lee held the Title three times and the length of her reigns totalled more than 400 days. Her first run lasted 295 days, a record for the Championship at the time.

9 BETH PHOENIX

Beth Phoenix, the "Glamazon," brought incredible strength and power to the Women's Division of WWE from 2006 through 2012. During that five-year period, Phoenix won WWE Women's Championship three times and the Divas Championship once.

10 CHARLOTTE FLAIR

Charlotte won the NXT Women's Championship in 2014. Moving up to *RAW*, she ended Nikki Bella's 300-day Divas Championship reign and retained the Title as it was retitled the WWE Women's Championship. She held it three more times in 2016.

TOP 10 FIRST CHAMPIONS

A CHAMPIONSHIP MAY be held by many different Superstars over the course of its history. But only one competitor can claim the prime distinction of being its very first champion.

1 — 12.9.2001

CHRIS JERICHO
UNDISPUTED CHAMPIONSHIP

After WWE purchased WCW, the World Championships were combined into one Undisputed Championship. Chris Jericho beat The Rock and Stone Cold Steve Austin on the same night to gain the Title.

2 — 9.1.1979

PAT PATTERSON
WWE INTERCONTINENTAL CHAMPIONSHIP

When WWE North American Heavyweight Champion Pat Patterson won a tournament in Brazil featuring several international champions, WWE created the Intercontinental Championship to reflect this achievement.

3 — 10.27.1991

BRIAN PILLMAN
WWE LIGHT HEAVYWEIGHT CHAMPIONSHIP

WCW created a new championship to recognize the high-flying, high-risk exploits of their Light Heavyweight competitors. Agile competitor Brian Pillman was the first Superstar to hold the Title when he beat Richard Morton.

4 — 2.26.1997

THE BRITISH BULLDOG
WWE EUROPEAN CHAMPIONSHIP

Throughout the history of the WWE European Championship, only two native Europeans held the title. The first champion, The British Bulldog, hailed from Leeds, England, and he first won the title in Berlin, Germany.

5 — 4.25.1992

JIMMY "SUPERFLY" SNUKA
EASTERN CHAMPIONSHIP WRESTLING

Before it was known as Extreme Championship Wrestling (ECW), the "E" in ECW stood for Eastern. The first Superstar to hold the title was WWE Hall of Famer Jimmy "Superfly" Snuka.

6 MICHELLE MCCOOL
WWE DIVAS CHAMPIONSHIP

Since WWE's Women's Championship was contested by the female Superstars of *RAW*, *SmackDown* added the Divas Championship to their roster and Michelle McCool beat Natalya in a tournament final to win it for the first time.

7.20.2008

7 SETH ROLLINS
NXT CHAMPIONSHIP

Seth Rollins has won multiple WWE World Championships, but he will always be remembered as the first Superstar to hold the NXT Championship before he joined The Shield stable and invaded WWE.

7.26.2012

8 FINN BALOR
WWE UNIVERSAL CHAMPIONSHIP

When the WWE Championship became the exclusive property of *SmackDown Live* after the 2016 WWE Draft, *RAW* created the WWE Universal Championship and Finn Balor became the first titleholder at *SummerSlam 2016*.

8.21.2016

9 MICK FOLEY
WWE HARDCORE CHAMPIONSHIP

Not only was Mick Foley WWE's first Hardcore Champion, but some would argue the Title was specifically created to honor his distinct style of competing, making it unique.

11.2.1998

10 VELVET MCINTYRE & PRINCESS VICTORIA
WWE WOMEN'S TAG TEAM CHAMPIONSHIP

WWE honored female tag teams for just over five years during the 1980s. McIntyre and Princess Victoria held the Title for just over 18 months, until an injury ended Victoria's career.

5.13.1983

6

3

TOP 10 ECW CHAMPIONS

THE ECW CHAMPIONSHIP WAS A sought-after prize in the 1990s and from 2006 to 2010 when **WWE** revived **ECW** as a brand. Many hardcore competitors spent considerable amounts of time defending this prize, often the sum of multiple reigns.

Raven and The Sandman
ECW Championship
Match 01.27.1996

ECW World Heavyweight
Champion, Terry Funk

1 SHANE DOUGLAS: 2 YEARS, 5 MONTHS

Shane is the only competitor in ECW history to hold the Title for longer than one continuous year.

2 THE SANDMAN: 1 YEAR, 3 MONTHS

The Sandman held this Title on five separate occasions, a record for the championship.

3 RAVEN: 1 YEAR, 1 MONTH

Raven won his first ECW Championship in January 1996 and a second time in December that same year.

4 TAZZ: 9 MONTHS

Tazz held the Title twice; the first reign was an impressive eight months, the second a mere nine days.

5 CHRISTIAN: 8 MONTHS

Christian was a two-time champion and the longest-reigning ECW Champion when WWE ran ECW.

6 TERRY FUNK: 7 MONTHS

Terry Funk's first ECW Title reign came in 1993. He won the Title again four years later.

7 MIKE AWESOME: 6 ½ MONTHS

Except for one week in late December 1999, Awesome held the Title from September 1999 until April 2000.

8 JUSTIN CREDIBLE: 5 ½ MONTHS

Justin Credible ended Tommy Dreamer's ECW Championship reign on the very same night it started.

9 BOBBY LASHLEY: 5 MONTHS

Bobby Lashley's first Title reign ended with a loss to WWE Chairman, Mr. McMahon.

10 BIG SHOW: 5 MONTHS

Big Show was the first Superstar in history to win the WCW, WWE, and ECW Championships.

TOP 10 YOUNG CHAMPIONS

ANY ASPIRING SUPERSTAR strives to win championship gold, and some get there sooner than others. But rapid success does not guarantee future glory. For some Superstars, a title early in their career is the first item on a legendary resume. For others, it is a fluke that will never be repeated.

1 — 19 years old

RENE DUPREE
WORLD TAG TEAM CHAMPION

Dupree became the first teenager to hold a WWE title. He and his teammate, Sylvain Grenier, made up the French Canadian duo La Résistance, which won the World Tag Team Championship at *Bad Blood 2003*.

2 — 20 years old

DAVID FLAIR
UNITED STATES CHAMPION

While it was David Flair's familial connection to his father Ric Flair that was responsible for getting him awarded the United States Championship, the young Superstar did manage to successfully defend the Title for over a month.

3 — 21 years old

PAIGE
DIVAS CHAMPION

Debuting on *RAW* the night after *WrestleMania 30* in 2014, Paige was granted a championship match by an overconfident AJ Lee. The young Brit shocked the world by beating Lee to become the youngest Divas Champion in history.

4 — 21 years old

REY MYSTERIO
WCW CRUISERWEIGHT CHAMPION

Throughout his illustrious career, Rey Mysterio won the Cruiserweight Championship eight times. His first reign, which came in July 1996 against Dean Malenko, made him the youngest Cruiserweight Champion in WCW history.

5 — 21 years old

ESSA RIOS
LIGHT HEAVYWEIGHT CHAMPION

Essa Rios's first match in WWE was a title shot against Gillberg. The flame-haired Rios did more than survive this baptism of fire, capturing the Light Heavyweight Championship in February 2000.

6 HORNSWOGGLE
WWE CRUISERWEIGHT CHAMPION

Hornswoggle was surely one of the more surprising WWE Cruiserweight Champions in history (especially to Jamie Noble, the Superstar he defeated). The diminutive Hornswoggle was also the youngest in the championship's history.

1

7 BO DALLAS
NXT CHAMPION

Before making it his mission to turn the WWE Universe into "Bo-lievers," Bo Dallas was the third ever NXT Champion. The youngest man to win the title, Dallas held on to it for nine months in 2013–2014.

7

8 BIG SHOW
WCW CHAMPION

Competing in WCW as The Giant, the Superstar who would later become Big Show put on a big show to win his first World Championship in 1995. The appropriately named Giant defeated Hulk Hogan for the WCW title.

9 RANDY ORTON
WORLD HEAVYWEIGHT CHAMPION

At *SummerSlam 2004*, Randy Orton made history by being the youngest competitor to ever hold the World Heavyweight Championship. Part of a revered family of Superstars, the young Orton was no doubt completely unfazed by his early success.

10 BROCK LESNAR
UNDISPUTED CHAMPION

Debuting in WWE in March 2002, Brock Lesnar hit the ground running. In less than six months he reached the top of the profession, beating The Rock for the Undisputed WWE Championship at *SummerSlam 2002*.

③

1 BRET HART VS. MICHAELS
WRESTLEMANIA XII

3.31.1996

It took longer than an hour for Bret "Hit Man" Hart and Shawn Michaels to settle their WWE Championship rivalry. The 60-minute Iron Man Match ended in a draw, so it went to overtime where Michaels scored the deciding fall.

2 SAVAGE VS. STEAMBOAT
WRESTLEMANIA III

3.29.1987

The Intercontinental Championship match between Randy Savage and Ricky "The Dragon" Steamboat stole the show at *WrestleMania III*. Both competitors had a combined 21 near falls before Steamboat finally scored the pinfall victory.

3 MICHAELS VS. RAMON
WRESTLEMANIA X

3.20.1994

In the first-ever Ladder Match at *WrestleMania X*, Shawn Michaels and Razor Ramon climbed the rungs to claim the Intercontinental Championship. Razor grabbed the Title in this innovative match.

4 FLAIR VS. STEAMBOAT
CLASH OF THE CHAMPIONS VI

4.2.1989

These bitter rivals had a trio of spectacular matches for the NWA Championship in 1989. After winning the Title, Steamboat won a 2-out-of-3 falls rematch, even though his final pin shouldn't have counted because Flair's foot was under the ropes.

5 CENA VS. CM PUNK
MONEY IN THE BANK 2011

7.17.2011

Controversial Superstar CM Punk won the WWE Championship in his hometown of Chicago following a spectacular match against John Cena. Before the match Punk badmouthed WWE, threatening to win and leave the company, promises that he delivered.

6
BANKS VS. BAYLEY
NXT TAKEOVER: BROOKLYN

8.22.2015

Bayley had come close to winning the NXT Women's Title many times. In 2015, she finally claimed victory, defeating her nemesis Sasha Banks in front of a sold out Barclays Center crowd, the first arena-sized audience to witness an NXT event.

7
HART VS. BRITISH BULLDOG
SUMMERSLAM 1992

8.29.1992

British Bulldog challenged his brother-in-law and titleholder Bret "Hit Man" Hart for the Intercontinental Championship in London. Thousands of fans exploded with excitement when Bulldog, the local hero, won.

8
SIX-MAN HELL IN A CELL
ARMAGEDDON 2000

12.10.2000

Kurt Angle defended the WWE Championship against fierce competitors The Rock, Undertaker, Triple H, Stone Cold Steve Austin, and Rikishi in a Six-Man Hell in a Cell match. Angle overcame the odds and won this epic Championship Match.

9
VAN DAM VS. CENA
ONE NIGHT STAND 2006

6.11.2006

Rob Van Dam waited until the second *ECW One Night Stand* event to cash in his *Money in the Bank* championship opportunity to challenge the current WWE Champion, John Cena. Van Dam won the Title with a shocking assist from Edge.

10
STRATUS VS. JAMES
WRESTLEMANIA 22

4.2.2006

When Mickie James's idol Trish Stratus did not return her affection, she got her revenge by stunning Trish to capture the Women's Championship in her debut *WrestleMania* match.

WHEN A CHAMPIONSHIP title is up for grabs, the **WWE Universe can't wait to** watch. There is always plenty of action, drama, and often there are surprises in the ring as **Superstars meet for the biggest prizes in** sports entertainment.

TOP 10 TAG TEAM CHAMPIONS

WHEN SUPERSTARS PAIR up, their combined strength can push them to dizzying new heights. Whether they are temporary team-ups or more permanent pairings, these Superstar combos deliver compelling performances that offer twice the tension and double the drama.

1 THE ROAD WARRIORS

With their muscular frames, face paint, partially shaved heads, and spiked shoulder pads, the Road Warriors intimidated their competition before matches even started. The duo—made up of Hawk and Animal—was the first ever to win World Tag Team Titles in AWA, NWA, and WWE.

2 THE DUDLEY BOYZ

Eighteen championship reigns: that astounding statistic belongs to D-Von and Bubba Ray, aka the Dudley Boyz. The half-brothers won the ECW Tag Team Championship a record eight times and later went on to rack up further titles in WWE in a career lasting more than 20 years.

3 MR. FUJI AND PROFESSOR TANAKA

This pair won the World Tag Team Title three times in the 1970s. They often played dirty, with Fuji famously throwing salt in the eyes of his opponents to temporarily blind them mid-match.

4 THE STEINER BROTHERS

Rick and Scott Steiner competed all over the world, winning tag team championships in WCW, WWE, and Japan. Their innovative offense, including the back-flipping Frankensteiner, combined moves from their amateur wrestling backgrounds with powerful suplexes.

5 THE WILD SAMOANS

Afa and Sika won more than 10 tag team championships and reigned three times as WWE World Tag Team Champs. The 2007 Hall of Famers help train future Superstars at the Wild Samoan Training Center in Allentown, Pennsylvania.

6 THE HARDYS

Brothers Matt and Jeff brought a wild, high-flying style to WWE tag team competitions starting in the late 1990s, earning themselves the nickname Team Extreme. The Hardys won seven tag team championships during their time in WWE.

7 HARLEM HEAT

Brothers Booker T and Stevie Ray entered WCW in August 1993, and won their first World Tag Team Championship the next year. In a blistering five-year period, Harlem Heat would go on to win 10 WCW Tag Team Championships—a mark no other pairing in history achieved.

8 THE FABULOUS FREEBIRDS

While most tag teams are pairs, the rockstar-styled Fabulous Freebirds came as a trio. When they won the World Tag Team title in 1980, a special "Freebird Rule" was put into place that said any two members of a multi-member team could defend the Championship. This rule continues.

9 THE HART FOUNDATION

Formed in 1985, the Hart Foundation was for six years a leading tag team in WWE. In a duo managed by Jimmy Hart, the combination of Bret "Hit Man" Hart's technical skill and Jim "The Anvil" Neidhart's raw power enabled the pair to twice win the World Tag Team Championship.

10 EDGE AND CHRISTIAN

After cutting their teeth as members of vampiric group the Brood, Edge and Christian departed the group in 1999 to become a duo. Together, they won seven World Tag Team Championships, including the first two *TLC* matches in history.

TOP 10
WWE
CHAMPIONS

THE WWE CHAMPIONSHIP has often been described as the richest prize in sports entertainment, and its five-decade lineage continues to this day. Winning the WWE Championship immortalizes a Superstar's legacy—fewer than 50 men have held the title.

1 BRUNO SAMMARTINO

In 1963, Bruno Sammartino became WWE Champion and held the Title for almost eight years. The Hall of Famer won it a second time in 1973 and held it for another three years. During the more than 11 years Sammartino was WWE Champion, he fought challengers from around the world, including Hans Mortier, Ivan Koloff, and Billy Graham.

2 JOHN CENA

To date, no one has won the **WWE** **Championship** as many times as John Cena, which is why he has earned the nickname "The Champ." Cena first won the Championship at *WrestleMania 21* in 2005. During his 12 reigns as **WWE Champion**, he has battled an incredible list of the biggest Superstars, including Triple H, Edge, Shawn Michaels, Randy Orton, Batista, and CM Punk. Perhaps his most impressive Title victory came at *WrestleMania 29*, when he avenged his loss at the previous year's *WrestleMania* by beating The Rock.

3 HULK HOGAN

January 23, 1984 saw the birth of "Hulkamania" when Hulk Hogan defeated the Iron Sheik to capture his first WWE Championship. Over the next few years, Hulkmania ran wild as it became nearly impossible to wrest the Title from the grasp of his famous "24-inch pythons." The Hulkster held the Title six times in total.

4 BOB BACKLUND

In 1978, six years after joining WWE, Bob Backlund won the WWE Championship. He was WWE's standard-bearer for nearly five years until he lost the Title to The Iron Sheik in 1983. Backlund's second Title victory came 16 years after his first. He was inducted into the WWE Hall of Fame in 2013.

5 BRET "HIT MAN" HART

Hart reached the apex of sports entertainment in October 1992 when he defeated Ric Flair for the WWE Championship. Hart went on to win the Title four more times. His final reign ended in possibly the most controversial match in WWE history, *The Montreal Screwjob,* which ended in submission though Hart never actually gave up against Shawn Michaels.

CONTINUED

6 TRIPLE H

With nine WWE Championship reigns, Triple H is one of the most decorated champions of all time. He has shown amazing longevity, with a sixteen-and-a-half year span between his first Title victory and his last. In addition to his WWE Championships, Triple H has won the World Heavyweight Championship five times, giving him an incredible 14 World Championship wins.

"BECOME A CHAMPION LIKE STONE COLD STEVE AUSTIN."

STONE COLD STEVE AUSTIN

7 RANDY ORTON

Orton's first WWE Title was awarded by Mr. McMahon at *No Mercy 2007*, following an injury to John Cena that forced him to relinquish the WWE Championship. However, Orton lost the Title to Triple H immediately after the presentation. Later that same night, Orton was able to regain the Championship in a Last Man Standing Match with Triple H. Randy Orton went on to win the Title a total of eight times.

8 STONE COLD STEVE AUSTIN

Stone Cold Steve Austin won the WWE Championship from Shawn Michaels at *WrestleMania XIV* in 1998. Over the next few years Austin would win the WWE Championship six times—perhaps most memorably in two *WrestleMania* main events versus his rival The Rock. Stone Cold's final reign with the ultimate prize came in late 2001 when he topped Kurt Angle on an episode of *RAW*.

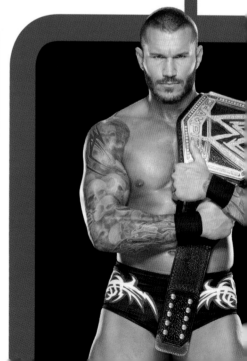

9 THE ROCK

At one point the record-holder for the most WWE Championship reigns of all time, The Rock's greatest Title victory might have been his eighth and final one. Over a decade after his previous Title reign, Rock returned to WWE and vowed to become Champion. He delivered on this promise at *Royal Rumble 2013* by ending CM Punk's dominant 434-day Title reign.

10 PEDRO MORALES

Pedro Morales only held the WWE Championship once, but for almost three years in the early 1970s. Morales was able to fend off challenges from future WWE Hall of Famers Ernie Ladd, Mr. Fuji, and George "The Animal" Steele. Two of his most famous Title defenses came against former champion Bruno Sammartino, but both bouts ended in draws that lasted over an hour.

TOP 10 DOMINANT CHAMPIONS

HOLDING A CHAMPIONSHIP is one thing. Becoming one of sports entertainment's most dominant winners is something else entirely. To do that, a Superstar must crush their challengers in such a convincing fashion that they leave no room for debate as to who should be holding the title. The only point of discussion should be their exact place among the all-time greats.

2003 WWE World Heavyweight Champion, Goldberg

John Cena won his 15th World Championship at *Money in the Bank 2014.*

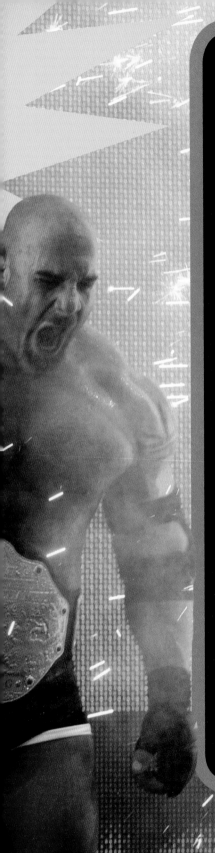

1 EDGE

Prolific winner Edge has won 17 singles championships, and also owns the record for most tag team titles: 14.

2 JOHN CENA

John Cena has kept his place at the top of the industry for a decade, becoming a 15-time World Champion.

3 BRUNO SAMMARTINO

After a Title reign lasting almost eight years, Sammartino held the WWE Title again for more than three years.

4 JERRY "THE KING" LAWLER

Lawler ruled the United States Wrestling Association, winning the World Title more than two dozen times.

5 BROCK LESNAR

Lesnar only lost the WWE World Championship at *WrestleMania 31* because Seth Rollins suddenly created a Triple Threat Match and pinned Roman Reigns.

6 GOLDBERG

After an incredible 173-match winning streak, it took an electric cattle prod for Goldberg to be defeated!

7 NICK BOCKWINKEL

Between 1975 and 1987, Bockwinkel held the AWA Championship four times for a total of eight years.

8 HULK HOGAN

Hogan gave his name to an entire sports entertainment era when "Hulkamania" ruled from 1984 to 1993.

9 THE ROAD WARRIORS

This feared tag team was a force to be reckoned with in AWA, NWA, WCW, WWE, and Japan, too.

10 CHYNA

Nobody could beat Chyna for the WWE Women's Championship—she retired still holding the Title.

1 NWA CHAMPIONSHIP (1986–1993)
WCW CHAMPIONSHIP (1994–2001);
WORLD HEAVYWEIGHT CHAMPIONSHIP
(2002–2013)

WWE CHAMPIONSHIP
1988–1998

2

3 MILLION DOLLAR CHAMPIONSHIP
1989–1992, 1995–1996, 2010

INTERCONTINENTAL CHAMPIONSHIP
1988, 2011–2016

4

5 WWE HARDCORE CHAMPIONSHIP
1998–2002

WWE CHAMPIONSHIP
2014–2016

6

7 STONE COLD'S SMOKIN' SKULL
WWE CHAMPIONSHIP
1998–1999

TOP 10
CHAMPIONSHIP
TITLES

▲ 8 WWE CHAMPIONSHIP
1964–1971

▲ 9 UNITED STATES CHAMPIONSHIP
2004–2005

▲ 10 WWE CHAMPIONSHIP
1963

THROUGHOUT WWE'S long history, champions have worn their trophies to show the world that they are the best. Over the years, the style of championship titles has varied greatly.

TOP 10 CRUISERWEIGHT CHAMPIONS

BETWEEN 1991 AND 2007, competitors weighing less than 225 pounds sought the title of the Cruiserweight Championship. Many of the matches featured high-flying competitors executing dangerous aerial maneuvers. The title was retired in 2007, and later reinstated in September 2016 as part of *Monday Night RAW.*

1 REY MYSTERIO

No one won the Cruiserweight Championship as often as Rey Mysterio. Rey's record-breaking eighth, and final, Championship reign came in June 2004 when he defeated Chavo Classic. Mysterio held his final Cruiserweight Title for six weeks before losing it to Spike Dudley in July of 2004.

2 GREGORY HELMS

Helms held the Cruiserweight Championship three separate times. During his third and final reign, Helms held the Title for a record 385 days—the longest Cruiserweight Championship reign in history. He eventually lost the Title to Chavo Guerrero in February 2007.

3 CHAVO GUERRERO

In contrast to his six reigns as Cruiserweight Champion, Chavo suffered a notable loss when his father, Chavo Classic, defeated him for the Title in May 2004, just four days after Guerrero had won the Title for the fourth time.

4 BILLY KIDMAN

Billy Kidman was one of the most talented Cruiserweights in both WCW and WWE history. The seven-time Cruiserweight Championship holder first won the Title in September 1998, and won it for the last time at *Survivor Series* against Jamie Noble in November 2002.

5 JUVENTUD GUERRERA

A five-time Cruiserweight Champion, Guerrera won the Title an impressive three times between January and November 1998. After a seven-year break from the Championship, Guerrera returned in 2005, successfully defeating fellow cruiserweight Superstar Nunzio twice to win two more titles.

6 JAMIE NOBLE

Jamie Noble had one of the most dominant reigns with the Cruiserweight Championship. Noble defeated The Hurricane for the title at *King of the Ring 2002*, and held it for almost five months before losing it to Billy Kidman at *Survivor Series* in November 2002.

2

7 TAJIRI

Known as the Japanese Buzzsaw, Tajiri held the Cruiserweight Championship three times between October 2001 and December 2003. In addition to the Cruiserweight Title, Tajiri also held the WWE Light Heavyweight Championship on one occasion.

1

8 CHRIS JERICHO

Chris Jericho was a four-time Cruiserweight Champion. During just one year, between June 1997 and June 1998, Jericho battled several of the greatest cruiserweights in WCW for the Championship, including Eddie Guerrero, Dean Malenko, Rey Mysterio, and Syxx.

9 X-PAC

X-Pac held the Cruiserweight Championship only once by beating the multi-time Cruiserweight Champion Billy Kidman in July 2001. The rivalry between the two Superstars did not end there, and Kidman won the Title back in October 2001—73 days after X-Pac took it from him.

10 DEAN MALENKO

Four-time Cruiserweight Champion Dean Malenko was lauded as "The Man of 1,000 Holds." He also won the Title disguised as Ciclope in 1998, but was forced to relinquish it when rival Chris Jericho argued that he hadn't signed on to fight Malenko.

TOP 10 WRESTLING ROYALTY

SOME SUPERSTARS LET success go to their heads, and they want to be treated like royalty in the ring. They demand respect—and the royal treatment—from everyone they encounter.

1 JERRY "THE KING" LAWLER

Throughout the history of sports entertainment, many men have claimed to be the King, but Jerry Lawler's claim to the throne might be the strongest. Lawler won the USWA Title more than two dozen times before taking his kingly crown to WWE, where he has been an enduring personality.

2 "MACHO KING" SAVAGE

In addition to winning the 1987 King of the Ring, Randy Savage defeated "Hacksaw" Jim Duggan to be coronated "King of the WWE". The Macho King ruled over WWE for more than a year with his manager, Sensational Sherri, who became known as Queen Sherri.

3 KING BOOKER

The 2006 "King of the Ring", King Booker, embraced his royal achievement like no one in history. Booker reinvented his entire persona, even adopting an English accent. He also assembled a royal court with Queen Sharmell, Sir William Regal, and Sir Finlay.

4 THE BILLION DOLLAR PRINCESS

As WWE continued its incredible growth in the early 2000s, the McMahon family saw the company's wealth explode. As the daughter of WWE's highest authority, Mr. McMahon, Stephanie McMahon earned the moniker "The Billion Dollar Princess."

5 KING CURTIS IAUKEA

Competing all over the world, Hawaiian Superstar King Curtis won more than two dozen championships, including WWE's World Tag Team Championship with Baron Mikel Scicluna.

6 OWEN, THE KING OF HARTS

Owen Hart's brother, the accomplished Superstar Bret Hart, did not openly brag about being "King of the Ring" after he'd won the Title for the second time in 1993. But Owen Hart proudly declared himself King of the Harts after winning the *King of the Ring* tournament in 1994.

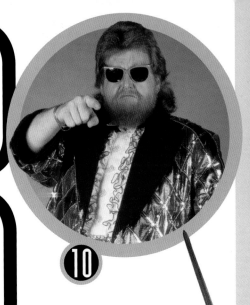

(10)

7 KING HARLEY RACE

After winning the 1986 *King of the Ring* tournament, Harley Race became the first WWE "king" to take the achievement literally. He began wearing a cape and forcing opponents to bow and kneel before him.

8 FRANCINE, THE "QUEEN OF EXTREME"

From 1995 to 2001, Francine was a fixture on ECW events, managing numerous ECW Champions, including Shane Douglas, Tommy Dreamer, and Justin Credible.

(9)

9 KING MABEL

The phrase "king sized" might have been coined just for Mabel. This once affable Superstar became a tyrant following his 1995 *King of the Ring* win, even tasking his jesters with carrying his bulk to the ring.

10 SIR OLIVER HUMPERDINK

A successful manager in NWA, WWE, and AWA, Sir Oliver Humperdink guided the careers of numerous Superstars, including Bam Bam Bigelow, Paul Orndorff, and the One Man Gang.

TOP 10 MOST ODDLY PAIRED TAG TEAMS

MOST TAG TEAMS IN WWE have been well-matched. Teammates share styles, interests, or may even be related. However, there have also been dysfunctional tag teams made up of Superstars who can't stand each other or who have absolutely nothing in common.

1 STONE COLD STEVE AUSTIN & DUDE LOVE

Stone Cold Steve Austin didn't want to team with Mick Foley's Mankind persona to defend the World Tag Team Championship. So, Mick Foley debuted as Dude Love, a freewheeling cool character who Austin could stomach and the pair won the Title.

2 BRET "HIT MAN" HART & GOLDBERG

Hart and Goldberg had little in common other than wanting to beat each other on the way to the WCW Championship. But the duo managed to put their differences aside, joining forces to win the WCW Tag Team Championship in December 1999.

3 TOMMY DREAMER & RAVEN

Despite being involved in one of the most bitter rivalries in sports entertainment history, Tommy Dreamer and Raven came together to defeat the Dudley Boyz for the ECW Tag Team Championship, a Title that they would hold together for more than four months.

4 TEAM HELL NO (KANE & DANIEL BRYAN)

Complete opposites, the demonic Kane and popular Daniel Bryan combined to form Team Hell No. Things didn't start out well and the teammates had to see an anger management counselor before competing.

5 CACTUS JACK & MIKEY WHIPWRECK

When Cactus Jack needed a replacement for Terry Funk in his ECW Tag Team Championship Match, the smaller Mikey Whipwreck seemed an unlikely teammate. But Whipwreck proved himself capable and they won the Championship twice.

6 SHEAMUS & CESARO

RAW General Manager Mick Foley gave Sheamus and Cesaro a chance to prove they were championship worthy by putting the duo in a seven-match series against each other. The series ended in a tie, so Foley forced the duo to team up and challenge for the World Tag Team Championship.

7 EUGENE & WILLIAM REGAL

William Regal was asked by *RAW* General Manager, Eric Bischoff, to watch over Bischoff's nephew, Eugene. After learning that Eugene was a WWE expert, the pair officially teamed up to vie for the World Tag Team Championship, which they won.

8 DARK CARNIVAL (THE GREAT MUTA & VAMPIRO)

Japanese legend The Great Muta shocked fans when he paired with the strange and wicked Vampiro to form Dark Carnival. However, the mismatched duo won the WCW World Tag Team Championship in August 2000.

DANIEL BRYAN

④

"I DON'T HAVE ANGER MANAGEMENT ISSUES."

9 THE GANGSTANATORS (NEW JACK & JOHN KRONUS)

For years, the Gangstas and the Eliminators were intense tag team rivals in ECW. But when their partners left ECW, former Gangsta New Jack and Eliminator John Kronos joined together to form the championship-winning Gangstanators.

10 BATISTA & REY MYSTERIO

The powerful Batista and the high-flying Rey Mysterio seemed unlikely friends, even when they were winning the WWE Tag Team Championship. The union eventually did dissolve when Batista unleashed a vicious attack on Mysterio.

TOP 10 TERRIFIC TOURNAMENTS

THERE'S NOTHING TOUGHER than competing in a series of rapid-fire matches. It's a fail-safe way to test a Superstar's stamina. In a tournament, Superstars give all they've got to go the distance and claim a title. With participant numbers up to a massive 32, fans can expect feats of endurance, jaw-dropping moves, and plenty of controversy.

CHARLOTTE
NXT Women's Championship Tournament
05.29.2014

Bret "Hit Man" Hart was crowned "King of the Ring" on June 13, 1993.

1 WWE CHAMPIONSHIP TOURNAMENT [Survivor Series 1998]

A vacated Title necessitated a one-day Deadly Games tournament, which saw The Rock crowned "Corporate Champion."

2 WWE CHAMPIONSHIP TOURNAMENT [WrestleMania IV, 1988]

After Andre the Giant's reign as WWE Champion abruptly ended, WWE held a 14-man tournament. Randy Savage claimed the Title.

3 SECOND ANNUAL CROCKETT CUP [1987]

Dusty Rhodes and Nikita Koloff (known as the Superpowers) beat 24 teams to win the tag team tournament.

4 NWA TITLE TOURNAMENT [1994]

This eight-man tournament had exciting matches, but it's remembered for Shane Douglas' refusal to accept the title he'd just won.

5 NWA TAG TEAM TOURNAMENT [1992]

Superstars Steve Williams and Terry Gordy beat 16 pairs from around the world to claim the NWA Tag Team Championship.

6 KING OF THE RING [1993]

The first time this pay-per-view event was held, Bret "Hit Man" Hart defeated Razor Ramon, Mr. Perfect, and Bam Bam Bigelow.

7 NXT WOMEN'S CHAMPIONSHIP TOURNAMENT [2014]

Charlotte defeated WWE veteran Natalya in the finals with her father, Ric Flair, and Natalya's uncle, Bret Hart, at ringside.

8 THE WRESTLING CLASSIC [1985]

Bragging rights were on the line at this 14-man tournament, dominated by the Junkyard Dog, who beat 10 Hall of Famers.

9 KING OF THE RING [2000]

This tournament was one of the largest in history, featuring 32 competitors. Kurt Angle won five matches to be crowned King.

10 INTERCONTINENTAL CHAMPIONSHIP TOURNAMENT [1990]

After Ultimate Warrior vacated his Intercontinental Championship, eight men fought for the Title, claimed by Mr. Perfect in the finals.

TOP 10 GREATEST LEGENDS

THE RICH HISTORY OF sports entertainment has produced many memorable characters. Among them are those who truly deserve to be called legends—those who have stood taller than the crowd, leaving a lasting impression around the world, and creating a legacy that has endured to this day.

1 BRUNO SAMMARTINO

Sammartino is perhaps the first of the WWE legends, having gained that status in the 1960s. He held the WWE Championship for nearly eight years—longer than any other competitor in history. A member of the WWE Hall of Fame, Sammartino remains one of the most beloved competitors of all time.

2 ANDRE THE GIANT

It would take more than a decade of competition before the mighty Andre the Giant would be pinned in a WWE ring. When Hulk Hogan finally accomplished that formidable feat in 1987, it was in front of the largest crowd in WWE history—a record that would stand for almost three decades.

3 CLASSY FREDDIE BLASSIE

Tough, flashy, and loud-mouthed, yet undeniably charismatic, Freddie Blassie would have been a legendary figure in sports entertainment either as a competitor or a manager. By performing both these roles so well, Blassie went down in history as one of the greatest of all time.

4 LOU THESZ

No competitor held the NWA World Championship longer than Lou Thesz, who reigned for a total of more than ten years. Thesz is also celebrated for his incredible longevity in the ring. He competed in seven different decades, making his ring debut in 1932 and fighting his last match in 1990.

5 ANTONINO ROCCA

A pioneer in the arena of high-flying wrestling, Antonino Rocca consistently headlined Madison Square Garden for seven years. Rocca's popularity was so great that in 1962 he was depicted on the cover of a Superman comic, hurling the dazed-looking super hero out of the ring!

6 GORGEOUS GEORGE

Competing from the 1940s to the 1960s, Gorgeous George was one of the first great showmen, using his flamboyant ring presence to gain national recognition in the early days of television. The well groomed Superstar left a lasting impression.

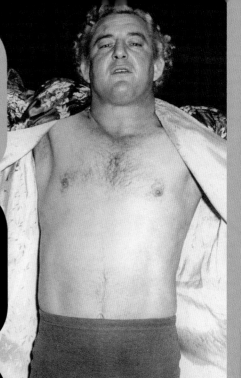

7 EL SANTO

El Santo was a titan in the Lucha Libre (traditional Mexican wrestling) realm of wrestling, competing in his homeland of Mexico for multiple decades. He also appeared in more than 50 movies, playing masked superhero roles. Famously, El Santo never removed his mask in public.

8 RIKIDOZAN

Considered by many to be the father of professional wrestling in Japan, Rikidozan was a former Sumo wrestler who crossed over into western-style professional wrestling. Korean-Japanese Rikidozan won multiple world titles in Japan, and a number of tag team championships in the United States.

9 MILDRED BURKE

Mildred Burke was a pioneering female Superstar, holding the Women's Championship for two decades against an onslaught of challengers, while also taking on—and defeating—male opponents. After Burke's in-ring career ended, she trained a new generation of female competitors.

10 ANTONIO INOKI

Antonio Inoki is renowned for two things: founding the influential company New Japan Pro Wrestling in 1972, and his famous wrestler vs. boxer match in 1976. The contest, which pitted Inoki against the legendary Muhammad Ali, ended in a draw.

1

BAYLEY

"I DREAMT ABOUT IT FOREVER."

4

3.31.1996

1 SHAWN MICHAELS

Heading into *WrestleMania XII*, for the second year in a row, Shawn Michaels hoped to win the WWE Championship, a title that had eluded him. He had to defeat the formidable Superstar Bret Hart in an Iron Man Match. Michaels won the bout in overtime, finally achieving his boyhood dream.

1.4.1999

2 MANKIND

For his entire life Mick Foley dreamed of becoming a World Champion, but through the years, despite entertaining millions as "Cactus Jack," "Mankind," and "Dude Love," he could never reach that elusive goal. On a January 1999 episode of *RAW*, he pinned The Rock to finally win the WWE Championship.

2.15.2004

3 EDDIE GUERRERO

Eddie Guerrero almost saw some personal demons derail his career as a Superstar, but he worked hard to overcome them and made it back to WWE. To further cement his return to form, he defeated Brock Lesnar for his first-ever World Championship at *No Way Out 2004*.

8.22.2015

4 BAYLEY

It seemed talented competitor Bayley could not win the NXT Women's Championship however hard she tried. She faced what could have been her final chance at *NXT Takeover: Brooklyn* against the acclaimed Superstar, Sasha Banks. Determined to triumph, she pinned Banks to win the Championship.

4.6.2014

5 DANIEL BRYAN

Arguing that he was a "B+ player," WWE bosses Triple H and Stephanie tried to prevent Daniel Bryan from becoming WWE Champion at all costs. They told Bryan he'd have to beat Triple H at *WrestleMania 30* first just to get a shot at the Title later that night. Bryan triumphed in both matches.

6 TOMMY DREAMER

4.22.2000

Tommy Dreamer was the heart and soul of ECW, but he struggled to win the ECW Championship. He reached the bittersweet epitome of his career at *CyberSlam 2000* when he finally won the Title from Tazz. But Dreamer lost it almost immediately to Justin Credible who challenged him to a match.

7 TRISH STRATUS

9.17.2006

Trish Stratus planned to retire at *Unforgiven 2006*, but not before winning the Women's Championship one last time. Trish won the Title and bid a triumphant farewell as she walked away from the ring in her hometown of Toronto, Canada.

8 RON SIMMONS

8.2.1992

Ron Simmons beat Vader for the WCW World Heavyweight Championship—his first World Title victory. He also became the first African American to hold the Championship, making his celebration even more emotional. His momentous victory was an inspiration to a generation of fans.

9 REY MYSTERIO

4.2.2006

The WWE Universe was stunned by the untimely death of Superstar Eddie Guerrero in late 2005. His friend, Rey Mysterio, took Guerrero's passing particularly hard. Mysterio dedicated his victory at *Royal Rumble 2006* and his World Heavyweight Championship win at *WrestleMania 22* to Guerrero.

10 RIC FLAIR

1.19.1992

Ric Flair had conquered the NWA, holding its world title a record seven times. But he desperately wanted to prove he could be the best in WWE as well. He did it in style, outlasting 29 men to win the 1992 *Royal Rumble* Match, his first WWE Championship.

EMOTIONS ALMOST always run high when a championship is on the line. However, some victories—whether for personal pride or fighting to maintain a legacy—mean more to competitors. These raised stakes increase the chance of something special happening in the ring.

SENIOR EDITOR
Tori Kosara

EDITOR
Pamela Afram

EDITORIAL ASSISTANT
Joseph Stewart

SENIOR DESIGNER
Nathan Martin

ADDITIONAL DESIGN
Anna Formanek, James McKeag,
Anne Sharples, Jaynan Spengler, Rhys Thomas

PRE-PRODUCTION PRODUCER
Marc Staples

SENIOR PRODUCER
Lloyd Robertson

MANAGING EDITOR
Paula Regan

DESIGN MANAGER
Jo Connor

PUBLISHER
Julie Ferris

ART DIRECTOR
Lisa Lanzarini

PUBLISHING DIRECTOR
Simon Beecroft

GLOBAL PUBLISHING MANAGER
Steve Pantaleo

VICE PRESIDENT, NORTH AMERICAN LICENSING
Jess Richardson

EXECUTIVE VICE PRESIDENT, CONSUMER PRODUCTS
Casey Collins

PHOTO DEPARTMENT
Josh Tottenham, Frank Vitucci,
Georgiana Dallas, Jamie Nelson, Melissa Halladay,
Mike Moran, JD Sestito

VICE PRESIDENT, INTELLECTUAL PROPERTY
Lauren Dienes-Middlen

SENIOR VICE PRESIDENT, CREATIVE SERVICES
Stan Stanski

CREATIVE DIRECTOR
John Jones

PROJECT MANAGER
Sara Vazquez

COVER DESIGNER
Franco Malagisi

CREATIVE WRITING
Chad Barbash, Dave Kapoor,
Ben Mayer

WRITTEN BY
Dean Miller

First American Edition, 2017
Published in the United States by DK Publishing
1450 Broadway, New York, NY 10018

Page design copyright © 2017 Dorling Kindersley Limited
DK, a division of Penguin Random House LLC

19 20 21   10 9 8 7 6 5 4
005–300000–03/2017

A catalog record for this book is available from the
Library of Congress.

ISBN: 978-1-4654-6264-0

DK books are available at special discounts when purchased in
bulk for sales promotions, premium, fund-raising, or
educational use. For details, contact: DK Publishing Special
Markets, 1450 Broadway, New York, New York 10018
SpecialSales@dk.com

Printed in China

A WORLD OF IDEAS:
SEE ALL THERE IS TO KNOW

www.wwe.com
www.dk.com

DK would like to thank Jon Hill for fact checking, Chantelle
Pattemore for proofreading, Sunita Gahir for design help,
and Dominic Aveiro, Matt Jones, Julia March, Ruth O'Rourke,
and Laura Palosuo for editorial assistance.

Photographs on pages 56–57, 59, 64, 159, 172, 180, 183, 197
courtesy of *Pro Wrestling Illustrated*.
All other photos copyright WWE.